SANTA BARBARA TRAVEL GUIDE 2024 - 2025

Your Ultimate Guidebook to Top Attractions, Must-Visit Places, Best Activities, and Budget Tips

Christy T. Davis

Table of Contents

Introduction To Santa Barbara

Welcome to Santa Barbara

Welcome to Santa Barbara, the American Riviera! Nestled between the Santa Ynez Mountains and the dazzling Pacific Ocean, this coastal jewel provides a slice of heaven that is difficult to surpass.

Prepare for an unforgettable trip down California's Central Coast, where the sun kisses the sea! This location is like a gigantic playground for sunbathers, surfers, and everyone who enjoys a good time under the blue sky.

Take in the pleasant feelings of this beachy beauty. Whether you're here to surf, eat fresh seafood off the boat, or simply walk about with the sand between your toes, Santa Barbara has everything you need to make your trip unforgettable.

So, put on some sunscreen, grab your sunglasses, and let's hit the exciting areas and hidden jewels of Santa Barbara. It's more than simply a location to go; it's a feeling, a mood, and a grin ready to happen. Welcome to the entertaining side of California!

Brief History and Cultural Significance

Santa Barbara Island, the smallest of the Channel Islands, is approximately thirty-eight miles from the mainland and is centrally positioned in respect to the other eight offshore islands. Surrounded by towering cliffs on all sides, the island lies alone in the sea, with only small Sutil Islet and Shag Rock to its southwest and northeast, respectively, for company. There are few beaches on the island, and those that do exist are frequently rocky and difficult to access. The island has a pastoral aspect, with undulating slopes and a large saddle between twin peaks, the highest of which stands at 634 feet. Santa Barbara Island is home to native seabird populations, barking sea lions, and a vibrant cultural heritage.

Native occupation and European Contact

Because of the scarcity of freshwater and terrestrial resources, Santa Barbara Island was unlikely to host any permanent native communities. Recent research has shown evidence that the island has been inhabited for at least 4,000 years, indicating that seasonal visits are common. Southern California Indians would have been lured to the island because of the abundance of marine life around the rocky shoreline, which allowed them to fish, collect shellfish, hunt pinnipeds, and create tools.

Because early European explorers left no trace of their arrival on the island, there is little information regarding native island use or inhabitants from those sources. Although the explorers visited the little island, little information was recorded about it. Cabrillo's chroniclers referred to the southern islands, including Santa Barbara, as the "other islands of San Lucas." Sebastian Vizcaino named the island after the saint whose feast day was December 4, the day he arrived in 1602.

Early History

Santa Barbara Island was acquired by the United States in 1848 and has been under US government ownership since then. Early government surveys conducted in 1853 and 1871 gave a topographic map of the island, and Signal Peak was named after a triangulation signal used at its highest point. Prior to 1909, there were no recorded leases on the island, but individuals did live there on occasion. In The Land of Sunshine, published in 1897 by J. R. Britton compared the island's profile to that of a camel, writing that "upon the higher hump stands the decaying beacon of the U. S. Coast Survey." He also noticed "a narrow shelf where a crayfisherman has built a hut of lath and canvas."

Heman Bay Webster, a fisherman and hunter, resided on Santa Barbara Island as a squatter in the 1890s. In 1896, he erected a cottage near the arch on the island's northwest tip, which is today known as Webster tip. In a 1940 interview, he described "abundant" cats existing on the island before sickness decimated their population. Webster was comfortable with the outdoors, traveling barefoot and having interests on other islands, particularly Anacapa, where he ran sheep. Other individuals also established Santa Barbara Island as a regular port around the turn of the century. Buster Hyder remembers Carl Jergensen and Bert Johnson spending years fishing for lobsters at Gull Rock (Sutil Island) in Thor, using a boat made by Hyder's father.

In 1900, the United States Department of Commerce and Labor began leasing the island for agricultural and recreational uses, promoting it for a five-year lease in coastal newspapers. J.G. On July 6, 1909, Howland, the highest bidder, got the first documented lease for Santa Barbara Island. Soon after, Howland subleased the island to C.B. Linton to propagate pearls in abalone. After five years, Howland decided not to extend his lease on the island.

The Hyder family

In the spring of 1914, public advertisements were again issued for a five-year lease on Santa Barbara Island. Two proposals were submitted, T.D. Webster of Carpinteria and Alvin Hyder of San Pedro competed for the lease, and Hyder won with a higher price of $250 per year on June 16, 1914. Hyder brought with him the island's greatest colony in history. Around 1915, the little island was home to around fifteen people, including Alvin's wife Nora and son Denton O., "Buster", as well as his two brothers and their spouses.

The year before the families arrived, Hyder and his brothers erected a residence on the island's edge, 100 yards south of and 150 feet above the landing. They secured the home to the ground using wires to keep the wind from blowing it off the cliff. Hyder restored the pier at the landing, where supplies and equipment were unloaded using a boom. To alleviate the strain of hauling items up and down 150 feet, he constructed a sled with wood tracks down the steep slope between the landing and the home.

Because the island lacked springs and running water, the Hyders built a network of reservoirs. They constructed two big concrete cisterns at the home and supplied water to Nora II from the mainland. In 1918, they built a Rambler automobile engine to pump water to the home from the landing. They investigated the island for water sources, including deep marine caverns, but were unsuccessful. Any collection method was employed, no matter how nasty. Buster described how "you had to limit your drinking water. It had to last a year. Then it got stagnant. Many times when it was raining, I'd drink water out of horse tracks. No kiddin'." Buster had the chore of cleaning dead mice from the drinking water source every day. "Boy, it was hard to drink it. But when you don't have anything else, you have to drink it."

In the early twentieth century, people made a lot of money farming rabbits, marketing the meat, and selling the pelts. Following the trend, the Hyders transported hundreds of pure black and white Belgian hares to the island and released them. They also brought roughly 300 sheep to the island in 1915, the first documented sheep to graze there before being fattened and sold for meat. The Hyders also had two horses, Dan and Charlie, and two mules, Jack and Beck, which they housed in a stable they constructed. Along with these animals, the Hyders raised goats, pigs, chickens, turkeys, and geese on the island.

The Hyders' lease ended in 1919, yet they kept on. After seven years of hard labor and misery, they decided to leave the island in 1922. They moved their twelve goats, 300 sheep, dogs, and four horses to their ranch in Cuyama Valley, north of Santa Barbara. They demolished the structures and transported the debris to the mainland in accordance with the lease agreements, but they did not remove the main home. Alvin Hyder reportedly attempted to renew his lease on Santa Barbara Island but was outbid by a Venice entrepreneur. Nevertheless, he returned 250 sheep to the island for fattening many years after their lease expired.

Government Activities in Santa Barbara Island.
After the Hyders left the island, various attempts were made to lease and develop resorts, but none were successful. No significant improvements were made to the island until the government constructed lighthouses.

As early as 1853, government personnel recognized Santa Barbara Island's potential as a lighthouse site. However, it would take 75 years to construct a navigational aid on Santa Barbara Island. On July 27, 1928, the Bureau of Lighthouses authorized an automatic light on the northerly point of the island "for the protection of inter-island navigation in general and particularly for the protection of the Hawaiian Island and trans-Pacific traffic, which follows a course passing six miles to the northward of the island." In 1934, a second light tower was built on the south end of the island, on the westerly side, located 486 feet above the water and visible for twelve hours. When Santa Barbara Island was designated as part of the Channel Islands National Monument in 1938, the government kept two parcels of property and the right of access for lighthouse operations.

In April 1936, the Commandant of the 11th Naval District sought authorization to place and maintain a rangefinder marker on Santa Barbara Island. The Navy erected a tower about 90 feet tall at the island's highest point, 634-foot Signal Peak, which was most likely destroyed by 1942, when the Army Signal Corps placed radar on the island. At the onset of World War II, the military ordered that both lights be temporarily turned out. They were re-lit in 1943, when the immediate threat to Los Angeles Harbor was believed to have passed. During the war, the Navy assumed responsibility for the U. The U.S. Coast Guard implemented a scheme of scheduled blackouts of coastal lights in the event of an enemy assault, as well as navigational aids. The Navy also established Coastal Lookout Stations on the island to help prevent assaults on the mainland.

Santa Barbara Island and Channel Islands National Monument

As early as 1932, the Bureau of Lighthouses proposed transferring Santa Barbara and Anacapa Islands to the National Park Service for protection. The National Park Service did not reply until 1938, when the island was included to the newly created Channel Islands National Monument, which also included Anacapa and Santa Barbara islands, on April 26. On June 28, 1939, National

Park Service scientists E. Lowell Sumner Jr. and R. M. Bond provided a study on the biology of the islands, recommending that the Coast Guard and State Division of Fish and Game safeguard the island and place signs informing visitors of the island's National Monument designation.

In 1949, the monument borders were increased to cover "the area within one (1) nautical mile of the shoreline of Anacapa and Santa Barbara Islands." On Santa Barbara Island, this meant that the stony beaches, offshore rocks, Sutil Island, and Shag Rock would all be preserved. In 1957, Cabrillo National Monument in San Diego took over oversight of the Channel Islands National Monument from Sequoia National Park. Rabbits and vandalism were serious issues on the lonely island, but by 1980, when it was designated as part of the Channel Islands National Park, the rabbits had vanished and vandalism was on the decline.

In order to better develop the island for tourist usage, the National Park Service built a new dock and ranger housing on it in 1991. Extensive habitat restoration efforts are underway on Santa Barbara Island to replenish native plant and bird species that have been decimated by years of rabbit and sheep grazing. Visitors may now camp, stroll routes around the island, snorkel, and kayak to enjoy the stunning natural environment that this little, inaccessible island has to offer.

Why Visit Santa Barbara

Santa Barbara, the city where land meets water, is one of those must-see destinations. The beachfront town, dubbed "The American Riviera" with good reason, provides something for everyone. Whether you live in the city or like the outdoors, you'll fall in love with this spot. And if you're still not convinced, here are a few reasons why you should visit Santa Barbara.

For nature admires.

1. Swimming and sunbathing

This Central Coast community is famed for its year-round sunlight, and you know what that entails. A day on the beach. Fortunately, you have a lot to pick from. Despite its tiny size, West Beach is a top choice for tourists. Santa Barbara's New Year's and Fourth of July fireworks displays are held here, which extends west from Stearns Wharf. East Beach, located east of Stearns Wharf, is the city's longest section of shoreline. If you're searching for dog-friendly beaches, head right to Hendry's Beach. This Santa Barbara must-see attraction allows your dog to swim freely without a leash.

2. Surfing and paddleboarding

Whether you're a seasoned pro or just getting started, Santa Barbara's beaches provide everything you need. Beginners learn to surf the waves at Leadbetter, where they can get all the guidance they need. But if you already know how to shoot the curl, head to Gaviota State Park or Jalama Beaches to experience the wild waves.

Not a lover of surfing but looking for something enjoyable to do? Consider stand-up paddleboarding. The wonderful thing about this activity is that you can perform it anywhere there is water, which includes all of Santa Barbara.

3. Kayaking

What better way to become familiar with the Pacific than to paddle into its depths? That's why kayaking is so popular in Santa Barbara—it's included in nearly every tourist schedule. Explore the diverse marine life, take in the breathtaking shoreline, and get your daily workout all at one. For the greatest views, start near Stearns Wharf and work your way down the wide beach.

4. Sailing

If kayaking is too much labor for you, consider sailing as a more relaxed alternative. Nothing beats sailing on a nice summer weekend, particularly around sunset. You'll have no problem picking up this activity either; there are lots of experienced sailors ready to share their knowledge. The finest place to begin your adventure is at the harbor. Head towards the picturesque beach and attempt to locate all of Santa Barbara's tourist attractions from a distance.

5. Whale Watching

As if there aren't enough reasons to visit Santa Barbara, whale viewing is at the top of every tourist's list. Over a dozen whale and dolphin species pass through the Santa Barbara Channel each year. Pods of enormous blue whales—the world's largest mammal—swim the seas around Santa Barbara. Condor Express offers the finest whale-watching and dining experience in the American Riviera—now that's a 'whale' day.

6. Hiking

Hikers know there are plenty of spots to explore in Santa Barbara for a good hike. One of the apparent explanations is the Santa Ynez Mountains, which provide a stunning backdrop to the seaside city. The mountains are teeming with hiking paths for all ability levels. Outdoor enthusiasts may enjoy stunning views of the city and the ocean— the higher you climb, the more rewarding the sights become. For those searching for shorter treks, Santa Barbara has plenty of oceanside paths and downtown strolls that will introduce you to new activities, maybe even undiscovered gems.

7. Historic Landmarks

The American Riviera has a rich history that has yet to be revealed. And where better to get your first history lesson than from the queen herself, Old Mission Santa Barbara? This Spanish mission is one of the most famous remnants of the 18th century. The mission, with its twin bell towers and stunning design, has earned the status of one of Santa Barbara's top attractions. Visitors come here to see the nine-room museum filled with historical artwork, spend a day in the lovely gardens, and pay their respects at the cemetery and mausoleum.

The Santa Barbara County Courthouse is another historically significant site to see. The Spanish Colonial Revival-style structure includes rooms covered in multicolored tiles, and the paintings fascinate tourists. What's the coolest aspect in the courthouse? The clock tower provides a wonderful view of the city and mountains.

8. Theaters

Want to receive a dose of art? Include the Arlington Theatre on your agenda. The Santa Barbara International Film Festival presently takes place at the theatre, which was originally built in 1931 as a movie theater. When you visit the theater, you'll be seated beneath a starry sky dome, surrounded by Spanish village decor that symbolizes the city's past. If Arlington isn't your thing, go to the New Vic and see a performance by the Ensemble Theatre Company. This location was once a church before being turned into a cutting-edge arena in 2013. The New Vic hosts both classic and new plays; get a pair of tickets to watch one for yourself.

9. Museums

One of Santa Barbara's most popular tourist attractions is the Museum of Natural History. The museum, which was built in 1916, exhibits many aspects of nature, from animals, birds, and marine life to fossils, astronomy, geology, and ethnography. It also features the Central Coast's sole planetarium. The Museum of Art is another popular tourist attraction in Santa Barbara. Located in the historic center, the museum houses some of the most important artworks ever created, including pieces by the great French impressionist Monet.

10. Restaurants

Who wouldn't like a superb dining experience in Santa Barbara? Your possibilities are virtually limitless, and deciding on one may be challenging. Toma Restaurant and Bar is an excellent choice for Italian, Mediterranean, and seafood cuisine. Try the incredible tuna cones and gnocchi with shrimp—they'll blow your mind. Brophy Bros is another seafood restaurant that offers a unique experience. Prepare to enjoy breathtaking views of the port, ocean, and mountains while indulging in delectable delicacies such as seafood pasta and seabass.

11. Shopping

Shopping in Santa Barbara is unavoidable—it's one of the most thrilling, relaxing, and yet stressful activities you can do on vacation. Shopaholics must first visit State Street, because shopping here is more than simply purchasing items; it is also a kind of tourism in Santa

Barbara. The Boulevard is dotted with cafés, restaurants, surf shops, and, of course, some of the greatest shopping in town.

If you're still looking for more shopping opportunities, visit Arlington and De La Guerra Plazas. For those wishing to buy souvenirs, head right to Stearns Wharf or Santa Barbara Harbor, where you'll discover adorable items to take home.

Chapter 1: Planning Your Trip, Getting There and Getting Around.

Best Time to Visit

Santa Barbara's moderate, Mediterranean climate makes it a terrific visit year-round, but particular times of year provide distinct benefits based on your choices for weather, activities, and crowd levels.

Spring (March-May):
Springtime is one of the greatest times to visit Santa Barbara. The weather is beautiful, the flowers are in full bloom, and the crowds are smaller than they were over the summer. It's ideal for outdoor activities like hiking, riding, and seeing the city's lovely gardens and parks. In addition, you may attend the Santa Barbara Earth Day

Festival, one of the largest and longest-running Earth Day events in the country.

Summer (June-August):

Summer is the busiest tourist season in Santa Barbara. The weather is warm and bright, perfect for beach activities, water sports, and exploring the vivid outside landscape. Events such as the Summer Solstice Celebration and the Old Spanish Days Fiesta attract enormous audiences and create a joyful mood in the city. However, expect increased costs and bigger people around this period.

Fall (September through November):

Fall is another fantastic time to visit. The weather continues warm, and summer crowds begin to disappear. It's harvest season in the surrounding Santa Ynez Valley, making it an ideal time for wine connoisseurs to tour wineries and sample wines. The Santa Barbara Harbor & Seafood Festival, held in October, is a highlight for seafood aficionados.

Winter (December-February):

Santa Barbara's winters are warm and pleasant in comparison to many other areas. Although it is the rainy season, the rain is usually mild, and bright days are still common. This is an ideal time for budget tourists because hotel costs are lower and the city is less busy. Gray whales migrate along the coast from December to April, making winter an ideal time to see them.

Whatever time of year you choose to come, Santa Barbara's Mediterranean-style environment ensures that you will be treated to lovely weather practically all year. Just remember to carry clothing because mornings and nights might be cold.

Budgeting Tips and Money Savings

Santa Barbara is famed for its richness and charm, but there are ways to enjoy this gorgeous seaside city without breaking the bank. Use these budgeting advice and money-saving tactics.

1. Visit in the off-season:

Traveling during the off-season, particularly in winter (December to February) and early spring (March to April), can result in considerable savings on accommodations and flights. The weather remains decent, and you'll dodge the summer throngs.

2. Book Your Accommodation in Advance:

Secure your hotel well in advance to benefit from early booking savings. Consider staying in affordable lodgings such as hotels, hostels, or vacation rentals. Areas just outside of the city core, such as Goleta or Carpinteria, can provide more cheap choices.

3. Use Public Transportation:

Santa Barbara's public transit system, which includes buses and shuttles, is both convenient and affordable. The Downtown-Waterfront Shuttle is very convenient and economical for moving around the major tourist attractions. Biking is also a popular and reasonably priced method to explore the city, with various bike rental businesses available.

4. Enjoy Free Attractions:

Many of Santa Barbara's top attractions are free or inexpensive. Stroll down Stearns Wharf, explore Santa Barbara Harbor, or unwind on one of the many stunning beaches, such as East Beach or Butterfly Beach. Visit the Santa Barbara County Courthouse, which offers panoramic views from its clock tower. The Santa Barbara Public Library and Botanical Garden both provide free or low-cost admission.

5. Make Use of Happy Hours and Food Trucks:

Dining out in Santa Barbara might be expensive, but you can cut costs by taking advantage of happy hour offers at local pubs and restaurants. Food trucks and informal cafes provide tasty meals at a lower cost than gourmet dining. The Santa Barbara Public Market offers a choice of economical and delectable options.

6. Pack a Picnic.

Pack a picnic and enjoy Santa Barbara's natural beauty. Shop for fresh vegetables and local delights at the Santa Barbara Farmers Market, which is open on various days of the week, then eat in a lovely location such as the Mission Rose Garden or Shoreline Park.

7. Apply Discount Passes and Coupons:

Look for bargain passes that include many attractions at a lesser cost. Websites like Groupon frequently offer discounts on local activities, restaurants, and excursions. Check the Santa Barbara Visitor Center for any current discounts or promotions.

8. Discover Local Events and Festivals:

Santa Barbara presents a variety of free or low-cost events and festivals throughout the year. Summer Solstice Celebrations, outdoor concerts, and community gatherings may all provide entertainment and cultural experiences at a reasonable cost.

9. DIY Tours:

Instead of scheduling pricey guided excursions, try conducting your own study and exploration. Walking tours, self-guided vehicle tours, and the use of apps or internet resources may all give valuable experiences for little or no expense.

By planning ahead of time and using these budgeting ideas, you may enjoy everything Santa Barbara has to offer while keeping your costs under control.

Visa and entry requirements.

Santa Barbara is a city in the state of California, thus the visa and entrance procedures are the same as those for the United States.

Visa requirements

1. Visa Waiver Program (VWP):

- The Visa Waiver Program allows citizens of 40 nations to enter the United States for vacation or business for up to 90 days without a visa. Prior to travel, travelers must apply for authorization through the Electronic System for Travel Authorization (ESTA).

2. Tourist Visa (B-2):

- Visitors from non-VWP nations, or those planning to remain for more than 90 days, require a B-2 tourist visa. This visa is intended for tourists, individuals visiting friends or family, and medical treatment. The application process includes filling out the DS-160 form, paying the visa fee, and having an interview at a US embassy or consulate.

3. Business Visa(B-1):

- A B-1 visa is necessary for business visitors to the United States who are not qualified for the VWP. The procedure is comparable to the B-2 visa.

4. Students and Exchange Visitors (F/J Visas):

- If you are a student or exchange visitor, you will require a F or J visa. Before you apply, make sure you've been accepted into a program and paid the SEVIS cost.

Entry Requirements:

1. Passport:

- All travelers must have a valid passport. VWP passengers' passports must be electronic, with a digital chip carrying biometric information.

2. ESTA:

- VWP tourists must get ESTA permission before traveling. This application may be submitted online and must be completed at least 72 hours before departure.

3. Visaholders:

- Travelers on a B-1 or B-2 visa must submit their passport with a valid visa stamp.

4. Customs Declaration:

- All tourists must fill out a customs declaration form upon arrival.

5. Proof of Sufficient Funding:

- Travelers may be asked to provide proof of adequate finances to support their stay in the United States.

6. Returned Ticket:

- Visitors under the VWP and visa holders may be required to present proof of a return or onward ticket.

Before arranging your travel to Santa Barbara, always check with the US Department of State or the US embassy or consulate in your home country to get the most up-to-date and particular regulations.

Transportation Options to Santa Barbara

1. By Air

For those flying in, Santa Barbara Municipal Airport (SBA) is a quick 10-mile drive from downtown Santa Barbara and provides a fly-friendly experience with easy access from terminal to gate.

With daily departures and multiple nonstop flights to and from major hubs such as Dallas, Denver, Los Angeles, Las Vegas, Oakland, Phoenix, Portland, San Francisco,

Seattle—and now Atlanta and Salt Lake City (beginning June 2024), it's relatively easy and convenient to fly to Santa Barbara and experience the stunning beauty, delicious cuisine, and fun activities of The American Riviera.

The Santa Barbara Airport represents the area's relaxed attitude and unique design. If your trip to Santa Barbara begins and finishes here, you will arrive and go in a traditional Santa Barbara flair. But flying in and out is only a minor part of the SBA experience. The attractively built building includes a Public work Program that displays commissioned work, long-term loans of existing art, and rotating exhibits of regional art, allowing you to get one final taste of Santa Barbara's distinctive arts and culture scene as you wait for your flight.

Nearby airports

Los Angeles International Airport (LAX) is located around 90 miles southeast of Santa Barbara. The airport serves dozens of foreign and local destinations, with flights on nearly every major airline.

Hollywood Burbank Airport (BUR) is roughly 85 miles southeast of Santa Barbara and serves various domestic destinations via eight major airlines.

2. By Road

By Car: A typical California road adventure awaits! Santa Barbara is easily accessible via U.S. Highway 101, which provides a picturesque drive along the coast. If you're traveling from the north or south, this road will provide you with breathtaking vistas and easy access to the city.

Public Buses: The Santa Barbara Metropolitan Transit District (MTD) offers substantial bus service across the city and adjacent areas. It's a cost-effective method to move about and see the attractions without worrying about parking.

Shuttle Services: Many hotels provide shuttle services to and from key attractions. Check with your hotel about availability and timetables.

Bike-Friendly: Santa Barbara is extremely bike-friendly, with designated lanes and routes that make it simple to explore on two wheels. It's also a terrific way to get some exercise and fresh air!

Amtrak: For a unique experience, ride the Amtrak train to Santa Barbara. The station is conveniently placed, and you'll get to see some stunning scenery along the route.

So, whether you're traveling alone or with a party, you have lots of alternatives for arriving in Santa Barbara in luxury.

3. By Train

Traveling to Santa Barbara by rail is both picturesque and soothing. what you should know.

Amtrak Pacific Surfliner: This train follows the coast and provides stunning views of the Pacific Ocean. It connects Santa Barbara with places like San Diego, Los Angeles, and San Luis Obispo. You may get off the train right in the middle of downtown Santa Barbara, among beaches and hotels.

Amtrak Coast Starlight: For those traveling from further afield, the Coast Starlight offers a lengthier journey with connections from Seattle to Los Angeles. This route runs via Santa Barbara and provides a scenic ride over various landscapes.

Both trains arrive at the Santa Barbara Amtrak Station, which is conveniently located at 209 State Street, only a few feet from the ocean and downtown attractions. It's an excellent way to avoid traffic and begin your Santa Barbara journey from the time you board the train.

Local Transportation

1. Public transit:

Santa Barbara's Metropolitan Transit District (MTD) provides a dependable and convenient public transportation system. MTD offers multiple bus lines that serve downtown, adjacent areas, and other communities such as Goleta and Carpinteria. Buses operate regularly, with reduced timetables on weekends and holidays. The Downtown-Waterfront Shuttle offers an affordable and picturesque trip along State Street and the waterfront for environmentally conscious travelers.

2. Car rental:

Car rentals are widely accessible in Santa Barbara, with major rental companies such as Hertz, Enterprise, and Avis operating at the Santa Barbara Airport and several downtown sites. Renting a car is an excellent way to explore the city's suburbs, adjacent wine region, and gorgeous seaside excursions. Visitors may pick from a variety of automobiles, including sedans, SUVs, and environmentally friendly alternatives. Advance bookings are advised, particularly during busy tourist seasons.

3. Biking and Walking:

Santa Barbara is a bike-friendly city with a vast network of lanes, pathways, and gorgeous coastline routes. Local bike rental establishments include Wheel Fun Rentals and Santa Barbara Bike To-Go. The city encourages cycling with the seaside Cabrillo Bike Path and routes through downtown and parks. Walking is also a pleasant way to explore Santa Barbara, which has pedestrian-friendly streets, particularly in the historic downtown area, where attractions, shops, and restaurants are conveniently located. The stunning coastline and urban paths, such as the Douglas Family Preserve, provide enjoyable walking experiences.

Santa Barbara's numerous transit choices make it simple to explore and appreciate the city's beauty and attractions.

Chapter 2: Where to Stay

Luxury Hotels

1. The Ritz-Carlton Bacara in Santa Barbara:

The Ritz-Carlton Bacara, situated on 78 acres of beachfront land, provides luxury suites with breathtaking ocean views. The resort offers magnificent rooms and suites, a world-class spa, three infinity-edge pools, and a variety of great dining options, including the iconic Angel Oak restaurant. Guests may enjoy exclusive beach access, tennis courts, and a wide range of outdoor activities.

2. Belmond El Encanto:

Belmond El Encanto, located in the hills above Santa Barbara, is a historic hotel recognized for its elegant elegance and superb service. The resort has well decorated bungalows and apartments with own patios and gardens. There is a relaxing spa, an infinity pool, and a gourmet restaurant with magnificent views of the Pacific Ocean. The hotel's extensive grounds and calm environment make it an ideal escape.

3. Four Seasons Resort The Biltmore, Santa Barbara: This landmark resort in Montecito mixes Spanish Colonial architecture with contemporary elegance. The Four Seasons has opulent rooms and suites, many with ocean views. Guests may enjoy the resort's two swimming pools, one of which is reserved for Coral Casino Beach and Cabana Club members only. Dining choices include the beachside Bella Vista and the vibrant Ty Lounge.

4) Rosewood Miramar Beach:
Rosewood Miramar Beach, located on one of Southern California's most stunning beaches, provides a magnificent coastal retreat. The resort offers exquisite rooms, suites, and seaside villas. Guests may enjoy excellent dining at Caruso's, unwind at the Sense Spa, or make use of the outdoor pools and workout facilities.

The resort's great beachfront position offers direct access to the sand and waves.

5) Hotel Californian:

The Hotel Californian, located in Santa Barbara's Funk Zone and the waterfront, mixes Spanish Colonial Revival architecture with modern Moorish-themed décor. The hotel has magnificent rooms and suites, a rooftop pool with breathtaking views, and a variety of eating options, including the famed Blackbird restaurant. The onsite spa and accessibility to local vineyards and art galleries make it an ideal location for exploring the area.

These luxury hotels provide outstanding rooms and services, assuring an unforgettable stay in Santa Barbara.

Mid-range Hotels

1. Hotel Milo Santa Barbara:

Hotel Milo, just minutes from West Beach, provides beautiful suites with a Spanish-inspired décor. The hotel has pleasant rooms and suites, many with seaside views. There are two outdoor pools, complimentary bike rentals, and a continental breakfast. Its great position provides convenient access to Stearns Wharf, the Funk Zone, and downtown Santa Barbara.

2. Best Western Plus Pepper Tree Inn:

This hotel offers excellent lodgings and a resort-like ambiance. Best Western Plus Pepper Tree Inn, located in uptown Santa Barbara, offers large accommodations with own patios or balconies that overlook lovely gardens or pools. Guests may use two outdoor heated pools, hot tubs, and a fitness facility. The hotel also provides complimentary shuttle service to surrounding attractions.

3. La Quinta by Wyndham Santa Barbara Downtown:

La Quinta is conveniently located on State Street and offers contemporary and comfortable accommodations at a reasonable price. The hotel has an outdoor pool, a fitness facility, and free breakfast. Its strategic position allows you to easily explore downtown Santa Barbara's shopping, restaurants, and sights. The Santa Barbara Museum of Art and the historic courthouse are both walking distance.

4. Brisas Del Mar, Inn on the Beach:

Brisas Del Mar, located just a few steps from the beach and harbor, welcomes guests with Mediterranean-inspired design. The inn offers large rooms and suites, some with kitchenettes. Guests may enjoy a heated outdoor pool, a hot tub, free bike rentals, and a daily continental breakfast. Wine and cheese receptions in the afternoon and milk and cookies in the evening are a nice addition.

5. Harbor View Inn:

The Harbor View Inn, which overlooks Stearns Wharf and the Santa Barbara coastline, offers well-appointed lodgings in a calm atmosphere. The hotel has big rooms and suites, many with ocean views. Amenities include an outdoor pool, hot tub, fitness center, and an on-site restaurant, Eladio's, which serves Californian cuisine. Its position provides convenient access to the beach, waterfront activities, and downtown attractions.

These mid-range hotels provide a pleasant and economical stay with good facilities and easy access to Santa Barbara's attractions.

Budget Accommodations

1. Motel 6 Santa Barbara, State Street:

Motel 6 is located on busy State Street and provides clean and uncomplicated rooms at an affordable price. The rooms are contemporary and equipped with basic conveniences. Guests may enjoy an outdoor pool and complimentary morning coffee. Its ideal location allows for easy access to neighborhood dining, shopping, and public transportation alternatives.

2. The Wanderer:

The Wayfarer, located in the bustling Funk Zone, provides a unique hostel experience with both private and communal beds. The resort has a shared kitchen, an outdoor pool, and a complimentary breakfast. Its stylish decor and convenient location make it a popular choice for budget-conscious guests seeking to visit Santa Barbara's art galleries, vineyards, and beaches.

3) Agave Inn:

Agave Inn, a tiny, family-owned hotel on upper State Street, offers colorful and pleasant accommodations at affordable prices. Each room is individually furnished with a Southwestern theme and has modern facilities like flat-screen TVs and mini-fridges. Guests may take use of free parking and Wi-Fi. The hotel is near downtown Santa Barbara and various local restaurants.

4) Super 8 by Wyndham Santa Barbara/Goleta:

This Super 8 hotel, located only a short drive from downtown Santa Barbara, provides cheap lodgings with basic conveniences. The hotel offers modern rooms with free Wi-Fi, continental breakfast, and an outdoor pool. Its closeness to the Santa Barbara Airport and the University of California, Santa Barbara makes it an ideal alternative for travelers.

5. Beachside Inn:

Beachside Inn, located near the Santa Barbara Harbor, offers affordable rooms in a good location. The hotel has pleasant rooms, some with ocean views, and facilities such as an outdoor pool, free Wi-Fi, and a continental breakfast. Its proximity to the ocean, Stearns Wharf, and waterfront activities make it a good choice for budget-conscious guests wishing to enjoy Santa Barbara's coastal appeal.

These cheap lodgings also provide travelers with pleasant and cost-effective alternatives, assuring a great stay without breaking the bank.

Unique Stays

1. Boutique Hotels

1.1. Kimpton Canary Hotel:

Located in the center of downtown, The Kimpton Canary Hotel provides a magnificent boutique experience with Spanish-style design, exquisite rooms, and a rooftop pool with spectacular city views. Guests may enjoy a nightly wine hour and use the complimentary bikes.

1.2. Simpson House Inn:

Simpson House Inn, located on a beautiful Victorian estate, mixes old-world beauty with modern facilities. The inn has beautifully furnished rooms and cottages surrounded by gorgeous grounds. Guests may enjoy a gourmet breakfast, as well as champagne and hors d'oeuvres in the evening.

1.3. Spanish Garden Inn:

This small hotel, with its Spanish-inspired architecture and modest setting, provides a peaceful respite. Rooms include individual balconies or patios, and the hotel has a tranquil courtyard, heated pool, and free breakfast.

1.4. Hotel Virginia Santa Barbara, Tapestry Collection by Hilton.

This historic hotel, located near the harbor and the Funk Zone, provides beautiful rooms equipped with modern conveniences. The boutique resort has a lovely lobby with a fireplace and is conveniently located near several attractions.

2. Bed and breakfasts:

2.1. Cheshire Cat Inn:

This beautiful bed and breakfast comprises two Victorian homes and various cottages. Each room is artistically furnished, and visitors may enjoy a full breakfast, afternoon wine and snacks, and well-kept gardens.

2.2. The Eagle Inn:

The Eagle Inn, a family-owned bed and breakfast near West Beach, provides comfortable rooms and suites, some with their own balconies or jacuzzi baths. Guests receive a complimentary cooked breakfast and may hire bikes to explore the region.

2.3. Secret Garden Inn & Cottages:

This charming bed and breakfast, located in a residential area, provides rooms and private cottages surrounded by lush gardens. Guests may enjoy a full breakfast, afternoon tea, and a relaxing, homelike atmosphere.

2.4. The White Jasmine Inn:

A White Jasmine Inn, located in a peaceful downtown area, offers individually furnished rooms across three cottages. The inn serves gourmet breakfast to guests in their rooms, as well as wine and cheese in the evenings.

3. Vacation Rentals:

3.1. Cozy Seaside Cottage:

This beautiful cottage, just steps from East Beach, provides a comfortable stay with contemporary conveniences, a private terrace, and ocean views. It's ideal for small families or couples seeking a coastal retreat.

3.2. Downtown Loft:

A trendy, fully furnished apartment in the center of Santa Barbara's downtown district. This holiday rental features modern design, an open floor plan, and convenient proximity to shopping, dining, and cultural activities.

3.3. Wine Country Villa:

This luxury property in the adjacent Santa Ynez Valley provides a one-of-a-kind experience with vineyard views, large rooms, and outdoor facilities such as a pool and hot tub. It's an excellent alternative for anybody wishing to experience wine country.

3.4. Coastal Bungalow:

This vacation rental is a beautiful bungalow in Santa Barbara Harbor with seaside décor, a private yard, and all of the conveniences of home. Guests have easy access to the beach, waterfront activities, and nearby food options.

Chapter 3: Must-Visit Museums & Attractions

Santa Barbara boasts a distinctive collection of museums and cultural attractions that are integral to the community. These venues teach, inspire, entertain, and even transport visitors back in time. Unique to Santa Barbara, they tell stories about the natural world, California history, architecture, art, music, and more. For such a small town, Santa Barbara is rich with high-quality programming, diverse collections, and aesthetic beauty at these fine institutions and landmarks, providing joyful, mind-expanding experiences.

1. Santa Barbara Zoo

Known as the "Zoo with a View" for its stunning coastal hilltop location, the Santa Barbara Zoo is home to over 500 animals representing 146 species of mammals, reptiles, birds, and insects. The zoo participates in global conservation programs to ensure species survival. Its manageable size adds to its appeal, offering a picturesque setting. Reservations are required for admission, with daily capacity limited. Booking in advance is recommended. Note that some animals have earlier "bedtimes" starting at 4:30 p.m.

Opening Hours: 9:30 a.m. – 5 p.m. daily; 10 a.m. – 3:30 p.m. on Thanksgiving, Christmas Eve, and Christmas.

2. MOXI, The Wolf Museum of Exploration + Innovation

The interactive MOXI museum is open to curious minds of all ages, featuring three floors of hands-on exhibits focused on science, technology, engineering, arts, and math. Visitors can explore seven tracks, including Tech, Sound, Fantastic Forces, Speed, Light, Interactive Media, and the outdoor Sky Garden. Timed reservations are required and typically open 30 days in advance.

Opening Hours: 10 a.m. – 5 p.m. daily; closed on Thanksgiving, Christmas Eve, and Christmas Day.

3. Santa Barbara Museum of Natural History

Founded in 1916, the Santa Barbara Museum of Natural History (SBMNH) has been a beloved destination since 1923. Nestled along a soothing creek on 17 acres of oak woodland, the museum is situated between Mission Santa Barbara and the Botanic Garden. A blue whale skeleton greets visitors at the entrance, and the museum houses 3.5 million natural history specimens, including Chumash artifacts and the region's only planetarium. Reservations are recommended but not required.

Opening Hours: Wed – Mon 10 a.m. – 5 p.m.

4. Stearns Wharf & Sea Center

An iconic Santa Barbara landmark, Stearns Wharf extends over the Pacific at the end of State Street. Completed in 1872, it now hosts seafood restaurants, a winery, shops, and offers epic views. The Sea Center, operated by the Santa Barbara Museum of Natural History, provides hands-on encounters with local marine life. Admission tickets are available onsite for the day of the visit. The Lil' Toot Water Taxi offers transport between Stearns Wharf and the Harbor.

Opening Hours: Santa Barbara Museum of Natural History Sea Center open Wed – Sun 10 a.m. – 5 p.m.; Lil' Toot runs 9 a.m. – 6 p.m. daily.

5. Santa Barbara Harbor & Maritime Museum

The Santa Barbara Harbor is a hub for aquatic activities, including whale watching cruises, scenic sails, kayak and paddleboard rentals, and fishing charters. The Harbor houses seafood restaurants and the Santa Barbara Fish Market. The Santa Barbara Maritime Museum (SBMM) offers dynamic exhibitions on tides, surf culture, marine conservation, and military history. The Outdoors Santa Barbara Visitor Center provides some of the best views in town. No reservations are required for SBMM.

Opening Hours: Santa Barbara Maritime Museum open Thu-Tues 10 a.m. – 5 p.m.; Outdoors SB Visitor Center open 7 days a week, 10:30 a.m. – 4:30 p.m.

6. Santa Barbara Botanic Garden

Set on 78 acres in the foothills of Santa Barbara, the Santa Barbara Botanic Garden is a living museum showcasing over 1,000 native Californian plants. Visitors can explore the garden's diverse landscapes, including a desert, redwood forest, and thematic terrains, along five miles of hiking trails. The garden also features a nursery where guests can purchase native plants. Advanced reservations are required.

Opening Hours: 10 a.m. – 5 p.m. daily; closed Thanksgiving Day, Christmas Eve, Christmas Day, and during special events.

7. Lotusland

Lotusland is a 37-acre estate in Montecito established by Polish opera singer Madame Ganna Walska in 1941. It is regarded as one of the top 10 gardens in the world, featuring rare collections of endangered cycads, a Japanese garden, prehistoric ferns, and more. Both self-guided and docent-led tours are available. Visits are by advance reservation only due to its residential location.

Opening Hours: Open by advance reservation only, Wednesday through Saturday between 10 a.m. and 1:30 p.m.

8. Casa Del Herrero

Casa Del Herrero, or "House of the Blacksmith," offers a glimpse into Montecito life in the 1920s and 1930s. This historic landmark estate and gardens span 11 acres and feature Spanish Colonial Revival architecture by George Washington Smith. Visitors can explore the meticulously appointed home and Moorish-style gardens on docent-led tours, which are by appointment only.

Opening Hours: Tours available Wednesday and Saturday at 10 a.m. and 2 p.m.

9. Rancho La Patera & Stow House

Founded by William Stow in 1871, Rancho La Patera & Stow House in Goleta is a historic gem featuring the first commercial lemon orchard in California. Visitors can enjoy self-guided garden strolls and docent-led tours of the Stow House, which delves into the region's citrus industry history. The 19th-century specimen gardens and redwood trees in Stow Grove Park offer a serene picnic spot.

Opening Hours: Grounds open from sunrise to sunset daily; Museum Store open Saturdays and Sundays, 1 p.m.- 4 p.m., with Stow House Tours at 2 p.m. and 3 p.m., Ranch Yard open 11 a.m. – 2 p.m. on Sundays.

10. Santa Barbara County Courthouse

The Santa Barbara County Courthouse, designed in Spanish Colonial Revival style by William Mooser III and completed in 1929, is considered one of the most beautiful public buildings in the country. The courthouse features a clock tower offering sweeping city views. While the interior is currently closed to the public, visitors can explore the stunning exteriors and the sunken gardens, and access a self-guided tour map online.

Opening Hours: Exterior accessible 24 hours a day.

11. Old Mission Santa Barbara

Known as "The Queen of the Missions," Old Mission Santa Barbara is the 10th of California's 21 missions and the only one continuously occupied by Franciscans. Its twin bell towers and distinctive architecture make it a renowned landmark. Visitors can take self-guided tours of the mission, gardens, cemetery, and chapel. The Mission Rose Garden across the street is also a lovely spot for a picnic.

Opening Hours: Self-guided tours available daily from 9:30 a.m. – 4 p.m.; Museum Gift Shop open daily 9:30 a.m. – 5 p.m.

12. El Presidio de Santa Barbara State Historic Park

El Presidio dc Santa Barbara, established by the Spanish military in 1782, is the birthplace of Santa Barbara. The 5.5-acre park includes historic adobes like El Cuartel and the Cañedo Adobe, which serve as visitor centers and house exhibitions. Managed by the Santa Barbara Trust for Historic Preservation, the park features meticulously reconstructed sites and period furnishings. Self-guided tours are available, with guided tours by request.

Opening Hours: Open daily from 10:30 a.m. to 4:30 p.m.

13. Casa De La Guerra

Casa De La Guerra, constructed between 1818 and 1828 by Jose de la Guerra, was the residence of one of the community's most influential figures during the Mexican era. Now a museum managed by the Santa Barbara Trust for Historic Preservation, it showcases original furnishings, rotating art exhibits, and displays on California's Hispanic heritage.

Opening Hours: Open Thursday through Sunday from 12pm to 4pm; exteriors accessible 24 hours a day.

14. Santa Barbara Historical Museum

One of the city's oldest cultural institutions, the Santa Barbara Historical Museum chronicles the region's history from the native Chumash people through the

Spanish and Mexican periods to Santa Barbara's role as a film industry hub. The museum features permanent and rotating exhibits and two historic adobes, Casa Covarrubias and the Historic Adobe. Admission is free, and reservations are not required.

Opening Hours: Wednesday, Friday, and Saturday 12 p.m. – 5 p.m.; Thursday 12 p.m. – 7 p.m.

15. Santa Barbara Bowl

The Santa Barbara Bowl is a 4,500-seat amphitheater set in the foothills, renowned for hosting legendary artists and bands in an intimate, outdoor setting. The venue's small size and scenic location make it a favorite among performers and audiences alike. The 2024 concert season runs from summer through late fall, with tickets available online or at the box office.

Opening Hours: Box Office open Tuesday to Friday 11:00 a.m. – 3:00 p.m.

16. Santa Barbara Museum of Art

The Santa Barbara Museum of Art (SBMA) is a world-class institution established in 1941. Its 27,000-piece permanent collection includes antiquities, Asian art, Latin American art, photography, sculptures, and 19th and 20th-century European and American art. The museum also hosts special rotating exhibitions, a children's gallery with interactive activities, and educational talks.

Opening Hours: Tuesday – Sunday, 11 a.m. – 5 p.m.; Thursday 11 a.m. – 8 p.m.

17. Alice Keck Park Memorial Garden

Alice Keck Park Memorial Garden, established in 1980, is a 4.6-acre botanical oasis in Santa Barbara. Named after philanthropist Alice Keck Park, the garden features diverse plant species, a large koi pond, and a sensory garden. Winding paths lead visitors through vibrant flower beds, serene lawns, and shaded groves.

The garden includes interpretive signage, picnic areas, and a gazebo for events. It's a favorite spot for bird watching and family outings, offering a children's area and various community events throughout the year.

Opening Hours: Open daily from sunrise to sunset. Admission is free.

Scan the above QR code for Santa Barbara Must Try Attractions

Chapter 4: Outdoor Activities and Adventures

Hiking and Trails

Santa Barbara boasts a diverse landscape perfect for exploring on foot. Whether you're a seasoned adventurer or a casual nature enthusiast, there's a trail waiting to be discovered.

1. Seven Falls:

Seven Falls beckons nature lovers with its moderate challenge and refreshing reward. This 3.4-mile hike unfolds along Tunnel Road, immersing you in vibrant greenery. As you meander through the lush landscapes, the anticipation of cascading cool water builds. The payoff awaits at the end of the trail: a series of serene pools perfect for a dip. Take a moment to soak in the beauty of the surroundings, the sound of the falls serenading you, and the cool water washing away any fatigue from the journey.

2. La Cumbre Peak:

For those seeking a more strenuous adventure, La Cumbre Peak stands tall at 3,995 feet, offering a challenging yet rewarding 10-mile trek. This route caters to intermediate hikers with a thirst for panoramic vistas. As you ascend, the surrounding landscape gradually transforms, revealing breathtaking coastal views. With every step, the anticipation of reaching the summit grows. The final reward? A stunning panorama that unfolds before your eyes, encompassing the vastness of the coastline and the vibrant tapestry of Santa Barbara below.

3. Inspiration Point:

Inspiration Point lives up to its name by offering a glimpse of paradise. Located 1,800 feet above sea level, this destination boasts stunning vistas that will leave you speechless. The beauty of this location is accessible by two routes, catering to varying levels of fitness. The shorter option makes for a pleasant 3.75-mile round trip adventure, perfect for those seeking a moderate challenge. Regardless of the route you choose, the reward at the top remains the same – breathtaking panoramic views that inspire awe and ignite the imagination.

4. Channel Islands:

For the truly adventurous, the Channel Islands National Park offers a unique opportunity to explore a captivating archipelago. Santa Barbara Island, with its low mountain peaks, provides thrilling hikes along coastal trails, all while rewarding you with incredible ocean vistas. Immerse yourself in the island's distinct ecosystem, encounter diverse wildlife, and lose yourself in the beauty of this remote paradise.

5. Lizard's Mouth:

Sometimes, a grand escape doesn't require a long journey. Lizard's Mouth offers a scenic reward with minimal effort. This quick and easy hike, just a quarter-mile walk off West Camino Cielo Road, leads you to a spot that lives up to its name. A giant rock formation resembling a lizard's open mouth sets the stage for jaw-dropping vistas. Pack a picnic lunch, relax amongst the beauty, and take in the iconic landmark. The panoramic views are so captivating that this spot is a popular choice for engagement shoots.

6. Rattlesnake Canyon:

Rattlesnake Trail offers a perfect escape for families, including your furry friend! This gentle 4.5-mile roundtrip hike is ideal for a day out in nature. The trailhead near Skofield Park leads you through shaded dips, revealing the captivating beauty of the canyon scenery. The gentle incline makes it manageable for hikers of all ages, while the shady paths offer a welcome respite on warmer days. Feeling adventurous? Take the Connector to Tunnel Trail for an extra challenge and a chance to explore a different section of the area.

7. Gaviota Peak:

Calling all serious elevation seekers! Gaviota Peak stands tall at 2,458 feet, offering a challenge for seasoned hikers. Located west of Santa Barbara in Gaviota State Park, the 5.9-mile loop trail promises a rewarding experience. Be prepared for a workout – the trail involves steep climbs, with a total elevation gain of 2,162 feet. But the effort is well worth it, as you'll be rewarded with breathtaking panoramic views of the Pacific Ocean stretching out before you. Choose the Trespass Trail for a more direct route, or opt for a longer loop via the fire road for a more scenic journey.

8. Cathedral Peak:

Cathedral Peak caters to thrill-seeking adventurers with a taste for rock climbing. Towering above the coast, this peak offers stunning views that stretch for miles, making it a coveted destination for experienced hikers. The strenuous four-mile roundtrip route is classified as Class 3 rock climbing, so be prepared for a technical challenge. Reaching the summit will not only reward you with breathtaking vistas but also bragging rights. Don't forget to sign the registration book near the peak to document your accomplishment. However, keep in mind that this challenging climb is not suitable for dogs, so leave your furry friend at home for this adventure.

9. Nojoqui Falls:

Nojoqui Falls beckons with its easy accessibility and hidden beauty. Nestled within Nojoqui Falls Park, this short but rewarding hike is ideal for a quick escape into nature. The 0.8-mile out-and-back trail winds through a cool, shaded path beneath towering oak and laurel trees. As you approach the end of the trail, the sound of cascading water intensifies, building anticipation for the reveal – a spectacular 80-foot waterfall. The falls are most impressive in the spring or after heavy rainfall, when the water plunges with renewed vigor. This easy hike allows you to witness a natural wonder in minimal time, making it a perfect choice for a family outing or a quick afternoon escape.

10. Santa Barbara Botanic Garden:

For a unique blend of hiking and botanical exploration, look no further than the Santa Barbara Botanic Garden. Located just three miles from downtown Santa Barbara, this haven for nature lovers boasts over 1,000 native California plant species waiting to be discovered. Imagine strolling through cool redwood groves, their towering presence creating a sense of awe. Wander through meadows bursting with vibrant wildflowers, each one a testament to the region's diverse flora. Scenic paths weave throughout the gardens, inviting you on a journey of discovery. Don't miss the authentic Japanese Teahouse and Garden, offering a tranquil space for reflection amidst the beauty. History buffs will appreciate the inclusion of the historic Mission Dam, a reminder of the area's rich past. Whether you're a seasoned botanist or simply enjoy a leisurely stroll surrounded by nature, the Santa Barbara Botanic Garden promises a delightful experience.

11. Los Padres Tunnel Trail:

For the experienced hiker seeking a challenge with diverse rewards, Los Padres Tunnel Trail is an excellent option. This popular trail, accessed from Tunnel Road, winds its way around the mountain, offering stunning city views as you ascend. The path takes you on a journey of twists and turns, revealing unique rock formations along the way. During the rainy season, the trail transforms into a wonderland of cascading waterfalls, adding another layer of wonder to your adventure. The average hike is approximately 7.5 miles, but ambitious hikers can extend their journey by continuing on to La Cumbre Peak. Remember to pack sturdy shoes and plenty of water for this challenging but rewarding exploration of the Santa Ynez range.

Water Sports and Activities

Santa Barbara's beautiful coastline and mild weather make it a water sport haven. From surfing to kayaking, the calm waters and stunning scenery provide something for everyone. Protected by the Santa Ynez Mountains, the beaches offer ideal conditions for all types of water activities. With sunshine warming the water and refreshing breezes, Santa Barbara's commitment to nature makes it a perfect destination for water sport enthusiasts.

Surfing

For surfers, Santa Barbara's beaches are a canvas of rolling waves. Beginners can find gentle swells perfect for catching their first ride, while experienced surfers can test their skills on more challenging breaks. Local surf schools offer valuable lessons and top-quality equipment rentals, ensuring you have everything needed to carve your own path across the Pacific.

Kayaking:

Glide across the tranquil waters of Santa Barbara and discover a hidden world teeming with life. Kayaking offers a peaceful way to explore the coastline, venturing into secluded coves and hidden inlets. Keep your eyes peeled for playful dolphins, majestic sea birds, and curious seals as you navigate the crystal-clear waters. The Paddle Sports Center caters to all skill levels, providing rentals, instruction, and even guided tours for those who want to delve deeper into the vibrant marine ecosystem.

Stand-Up Paddleboarding:

Stand-up paddleboarding (SUP) is the perfect way to combine exercise with breathtaking scenery. Imagine yourself atop a paddleboard, carving across the turquoise expanse, feeling the gentle rhythm of the waves against your board. Beginners can benefit from lessons with experienced instructors, mastering the art of balancing and paddling before venturing out on their own. The beauty lies in the versatility of SUP – explore the calm, protected coves or catch some gentle waves for a more dynamic experience.

Each of these water sports offers a unique perspective on Santa Barbara's stunning coastline. Whether you're gliding over the waves with the wind in your hair, navigating a kayak through hidden coves, or finding your balance on a paddleboard, one thing is certain: unforgettable memories await. For those seeking additional options, companies like Santa Barbara Adventure Company and Cal Coast Adventures offer a range of exciting water-based activities, from thrilling sea cave tours to personalized surf lessons. So, come and explore Santa Barbara's aquatic playground – the perfect destination to reconnect with nature and create lasting memories on the water.

Biking Routes

Cabrillo Bike Path:

This crown jewel of Santa Barbara's cycling scene is the Cabrillo Bike Path. Stretching from Leadbetter Beach to Butterfly Beach, this paved and flat route is a 4.5-mile delight for families and casual riders. Enjoy a leisurely cruise along the scenic coastline, taking in the ocean views and soaking up the California sunshine.

Stearns Wharf to Old Mission Santa Barbara:

Embark on a historical adventure with a bike ride from Stearns Wharf to the iconic Old Mission Santa Barbara. This roughly 3-mile one-way route takes you along State Street, offering a charming mix of cityscapes and historical landmarks. Pedal past bustling shops and restaurants, eventually reaching the grandeur of the Old Mission, a testament to the area's rich past.

Obern Trail:

Craving a serene escape amidst nature? Look no further than the Obern Trail. This well-maintained path winds through Goleta, providing a peaceful ride amidst a natural setting. The trail's moderate length makes it ideal for a refreshing workout surrounded by scenic landscapes.

Mountain Biking Adventures

For adrenaline seekers, Santa Barbara boasts thrilling mountain biking trails that cater to experienced riders. Local bike shops are equipped to assist you with maps, rentals, and top-of-the-line mountain bikes, allowing you to tackle these challenging adventures.

Wine Country Tours:

Explore the captivating beauty of Santa Barbara's wine country on a guided bike tour. Companies offer these unique experiences, complete with bike rentals, helmets, picnic lunches, and of course, delectable wine tastings. Imagine pedaling through rolling vineyards, the sun warming your face, before indulging in a delicious picnic and savoring the flavors of the region's finest wines.

Wildlife Watching

Santa Barbara is a treasure trove for wildlife enthusiasts, offering a rich tapestry of opportunities for wildlife watching:

1. Whale Watching

- The Santa Barbara Channel is a renowned hotspot for whale watching, where you can spot over 30 species of marine mammals, including majestic blue whales, humpback whales, and playful dolphins. The area's nutrient-rich waters attract a diverse array of sea life, making it an ideal location for guided boat tours.

2. Andree Clark Bird Refuge

- This 42-acre park features a 29-acre lake and brackish wetlands that provide a sanctuary for migratory and local birds. It's a perfect spot for bird watching, with walking and biking trails that allow for leisurely observation of the area's avian inhabitants.

3. Santa Barbara Botanic Gardens

- While not exclusively for wildlife, the botanic gardens are home to native plant species that attract a variety of birds and insects, offering a peaceful setting for nature observation within the city's limits.

4. Butterfly Watching

- Santa Barbara is also known for its monarch butterfly populations. The area participates in annual butterfly counts and provides habitats that support these delicate creatures, making it a delightful place for butterfly enthusiasts.

Chapter 5: Dining and Nightlife

Top Restaurants

Santa Barbara's vibrant restaurant scene caters to every palate, offering a diverse range of culinary experiences. From intimate kaiseki restaurants to lively spots showcasing global flavors, here are six exceptional restaurants to tantalize your taste buds:

1. Bouchon Santa Barbara: Indulge in an intimate fine-dining experience at Bouchon Santa Barbara. Established in 1998, this restaurant played a key role in putting Santa Barbara's wine country cuisine on the map. Expect French-inspired seasonal California fare with a warm and welcoming atmosphere thanks to proprietor Mitchell Sjerven's renowned hospitality. Their extensive

wine list showcases some of the region's best selections, making it a perfect spot for wine enthusiasts.

2. Toma Restaurant & Bar: A consistent favorite on OpenTable's "Most Booked" list, Toma Restaurant & Bar offers a relaxed fine-dining experience with stunning waterfront views along Cabrillo Boulevard. Their coastal-inspired menu features artfully crafted pastas, vibrant flatbreads, perfectly grilled fish and succulent meats, all culminating in a truly memorable dining experience.

3. Secret Bao: Don't miss Secret Bao, a hidden gem offering a delicious exploration of Asian-fusion cuisine. Their menu boasts a mouthwatering selection of bao buns, featuring fresh, locally-sourced ingredients. They also have rotating noodle dishes and seasonal dumplings, making it a perfect spot for a satisfying and flavorful lunch or dinner.

4. The Black Sheep "SB Brasserie: Embark on a culinary adventure at The Black Sheep "SB Brasserie,"

where French-California cuisine takes center stage. This modern pub-style restaurant sources its ingredients locally, ensuring fresh and bursting flavors in every dish. Savor their delectable filet tartare, crafted with the finest cut of meat, or their mouthwatering grass-fed beef burger on a potato brioche bun. Wash it all down with a perfect glass of wine chosen from their extensive list of local and international selections.

5. Loquita: Experience the vibrant energy and delicious Spanish tapas at Loquita, a lively dinner-only restaurant in the Funk Zone. Chef Nikolas Ramirez creates stunning interpretations of traditional Spanish cuisine, utilizing the abundance of fresh produce Santa Barbara County has to offer. The menu features a delightful selection of hot and cold tapas, seasonal paellas, and wood-fired grilled seafood and meats. Don't forget to explore their cocktail program, known as one of the best in town, featuring creative takes on Spanish classics.

6. Boathouse at Hendry's Beach: It's hard to beat the combination of stunning oceanfront views and delicious

food offered by the Boathouse at Hendry's Beach. This family-friendly restaurant caters to all tastes, serving breakfast, lunch, and dinner. Their menu features a diverse selection, ranging from classic comfort food like eggs benedict and fish tacos to juicy burgers and crisp wedge salads. Seafood lovers rejoice! They offer a delightful raw bar and a variety of fresh catch options.

7. Sama Sama Kitchen: Michelin Bib Gourmand-approved Sama Sama Kitchen brings a vibrant and contemporary twist to Southeast Asian cuisine. Their lunch and dinner menu features innovative dishes prepared with fresh, locally-sourced ingredients. Get ready for a delightful explosion of flavors unlike anything else in town.

8. Bibi Ji: This contemporary Indian restaurant has become a local favorite since its debut in 2018. Partners Alejandro Medina and James Beard award-winning sommelier Rajat Parr offer playful spins on classic Indian dishes and street food, guaranteeing a delectable

dining experience. Don't miss their signature Uni Biryani, a "local delight" featuring fresh sea urchin.

9. Convivo Restaurant & Bar: Convivo Restaurant & Bar is a crowd-pleaser with its creative Mediterranean-inspired menu. They offer a variety of wood-fired flatbreads and pizzas, house-made pastas, seasonal salads, and enticing small plates. Their prime location at the Santa Barbara Inn takes full advantage of the stunning oceanfront views, with abundant outdoor seating overlooking East Beach.

10. Barbareño: Experience the rustic charm of Barbareño, drawing inspiration from Santa Barbara's Chumash Indian heritage. This restaurant champions local purveyors, crafting thoroughly modern and high-quality Central Coast cuisine with a playful touch. Executive Chef Julian Martinez and Chef de Cuisine Preston Knox are the masterminds behind innovative dishes that feel both comforting and exciting, creating a truly welcoming neighborhood vibe.

11. Bettina: This charming restaurant is a haven for pizza lovers. Their wood-fired pizzas are legendary, featuring fresh, high-quality ingredients like hand-pulled mozzarella and seasonal farmer's market greens. Bettina's cozy and rustic atmosphere creates the perfect setting for a romantic dinner date or a casual gathering with friends, complete with refreshing spritz cocktails.

Local Cuisine and Specialty Foods

1. Fresh Seafood: Santa Barbara boasts a stunning coastline, making fresh seafood a must-try. From delicate Santa Barbara spot prawns to cioppino overflowing with shellfish, local restaurants showcase the bounty of the Pacific. Enjoy oceanfront dining or visit the Santa Barbara Shellfish Company for a casual seafood experience.

2. Santa Barbara County Wine: With a diverse range of microclimates, Santa Barbara County is a haven for wine lovers. Explore varietals like Pinot Noir and Chardonnay from the Santa Maria Valley or venture to the warmer

regions for Syrah and Grenache. Wineries often have tasting rooms, offering a chance to sip and savor amidst beautiful scenery.

3. California Avocados: California avocados, known for their creamy texture and rich flavor, are a staple in Santa Barbara cuisine. Enjoy them in guacamole, atop salads, or simply savor them on their own. Visit farmers markets to find the freshest local avocados at their peak.

4. Santa Barbara Sea Salt: Hand-harvested from the Pacific Ocean, Santa Barbara Sea Salt adds a touch of magic to any dish. Its unique mineral profile enhances the flavors of seafood, vegetables, and even desserts. Look for it in gourmet shops or visit the Santa Barbara Sea Salt Company for a taste of the ocean.

5. Local Honey: Santa Barbara's diverse flora gives rise to a variety of delicious local honeys. From the citrusy notes of orange blossom honey to the rich, earthy flavor of wildflower honey, there's a perfect honey to complement your favorite dish. Explore farmers markets

or specialty shops to discover the unique flavors of Santa Barbara honey.

6. California Almonds: California is the world's leading producer of almonds, and Santa Barbara County is a major contributor. Enjoy these versatile nuts in their natural state, roasted and salted, or incorporated into delicious desserts. Visit local farms or shops to discover the wide variety of California almonds available.

Best Cafes and Bakeries

Santa Barbara isn't just a city of stunning beaches and captivating architecture; it's a haven for coffee connoisseurs and pastry aficionados. With a thriving cafe culture, the city offers a delightful array of options, whether you crave a morning pick-me-up, a delightful afternoon treat, or a decadent dessert to cap off your day.

1. Helena Avenue Bakery:
Step into Helena Avenue Bakery and be greeted by the warm aroma of freshly baked bread and handcrafted

pastries. This artisan haven champions organic ingredients, transforming them into crusty loaves, delicate croissants, and mouthwatering breakfast and lunch creations. It's the perfect spot to fuel up before exploring the vibrant Funk Zone or indulging in a serene beach picnic.

2. Crushcakes & Cafe:

Craving a satisfying breakfast or lunch alongside a delightful pastry? Crushcakes & Cafe is your answer. Beloved for its catering services and from-scratch offerings, this cafe caters to both sweet and savory palates. Whether you're tempted by a flaky scone or a hearty seasonal salad, Crushcakes guarantees a delicious and satisfying experience.

3. Bree'Osh Bakery Cafe Santa Barbara:

Calling all Francophiles and pastry enthusiasts! Bree'Osh Bakery Cafe Santa Barbara transports you straight to a charming Parisian cafe. Their specialty lies in French pastries, each a delightful work of art boasting intricate details and the promise of exquisite flavor. From buttery croissants to decadent éclairs, Bree'Osh offers a taste of Parisian indulgence without the need for a transatlantic flight.

4. Handlebar Coffee Roasters:

Handlebar Coffee Roasters is a local institution, revered for its exceptional coffee and welcoming atmosphere. Their dedication to the craft shines through in every cup, offering a variety of expertly roasted beans brewed to perfection. Complement your caffeine fix with a freshly baked pastry or a delicious breakfast sandwich, making Handlebar the ideal spot for a vibrant and energizing start to your day.

5. Lilac Patisserie:

Lilac Patisserie caters to those with dietary restrictions without sacrificing an ounce of flavor. This haven of gluten-free delights offers a selection of delectable cakes and pastries that rival their traditional counterparts in taste and visual appeal. Indulge in a guilt-free slice of cake or a satisfying pastry, all crafted with the finest ingredients and a commitment to inclusivity.

6. Renaud's Patisserie & Bistro:

Renaud's Patisserie & Bistro evokes the charm of a quintessential French eatery. Their display of pastries is a feast for the eyes, featuring an array of croissants, quiches, and other delightful treats. Settle in with a steaming cup of coffee and savor the delicate flavors and textures, taking a moment to appreciate the timeless allure of French cafe culture.

7. Jeannine's Bakery & Cafe:

Jeannine's Bakery & Cafe, a local favorite with multiple locations throughout Santa Barbara, offers a warm and inviting atmosphere perfect for a casual breakfast or lunch. Their menu features American classics with a touch of creativity, ensuring there's something to satisfy every craving. Don't forget to explore their selection of pastries, a delightful complement to your meal or a perfect afternoon indulgence.

With each of these cafes and bakeries offering a unique experience, you're guaranteed to find a haven that speaks to your taste buds and preferences. So, embark on your own caffeinated journey through Santa Barbara's vibrant cafe culture, savoring the city's dedication to quality coffee, fresh ingredients, and delectable pastries.

Wine Tasting and Vineyards

Santa Barbara boasts a world-class wine scene, and you're in for a treat!

1. Urban Wine Trail

Start your exploration right in the heart of Santa Barbara with the Urban Wine Trail. This convenient option puts a cluster of tasting rooms at your fingertips, allowing you to sample a diverse array of local wines without leaving the city. It's a perfect way to dip your toes into Santa Barbara's vintages.

2. Santa Ynez Valley

Ready to delve deeper? A short drive away lies the crown jewel - Santa Ynez Valley. This picturesque region is where rolling vineyards meet rustic wineries. Immerse yourself in the breathtaking scenery and savor world-class wines while experiencing the warm hospitality of local vintners.

3. Sta. Rita Hills

Wine connoisseurs, take note! Sta. Rita Hills beckons with its reputation for exceptional pinot noir and chardonnay. Unique east-west mountain ranges create ideal growing conditions, resulting in these highly sought-after wines. Explore the wineries here to discover your perfect pinot or a refreshing chardonnay.

4. Ballard Canyon

If bolder flavors are your preference, head to Ballard Canyon. This region specializes in Rhône varietals like syrah and grenache, known for their robust and full-bodied characteristics. Prepare for a distinct wine tasting experience as you explore the wineries here.

5. Happy Canyon

Venture to the easternmost part of Santa Ynez Valley and discover Happy Canyon. This area is famous for Bordeaux varieties like cabernet sauvignon and merlot.

Explore the wineries here to savor these classic grapes and expand your wine palate.

6. Wine Tours

Want to fully immerse yourself in the wine country experience without worrying about driving or logistics? Consider booking a wine tour. Local experts will curate your day, taking you to exceptional wineries and allowing you to focus on enjoying the tastings and the stunning scenery.

7. Wine Festivals

Throughout the year, Santa Barbara comes alive with various wine festivals. These vibrant events showcase the region's diverse wines and offer a chance to meet the passionate winemakers behind them. Immerse yourself in the festive atmosphere and discover new favorites!

With this guide, you're well-equipped to embark on your Santa Barbara wine adventure. So, raise a glass and toast to a delightful exploration of this world-renowned wine region!

Bars and Nightclubs

Santa Barbara isn't just about stunning beaches and charming architecture; it also boasts a vibrant nightlife scene. Whether you crave a laid-back evening with friends or a night of dancing, there's a spot waiting to welcome you.

1. Wildcat Lounge:

If you're looking to unleash your inner party animal, Wildcat Lounge is the place to be. This high-energy club features renowned DJs, electrifying go-go dancers, and a state-of-the-art sound system guaranteed to get you moving. Prepare for an energetic night filled with pulsating music and dancing crowds.

2. The Neighborhood Bar:

Craving a more relaxed atmosphere? The Neighborhood Bar is your haven. This local favorite offers a laid-back vibe with affordable drinks, making it the perfect spot for catching up with friends, watching the game, or simply unwinding after a long day.

3. James Joyce:

For a taste of Ireland in Santa Barbara, head to James Joyce. This iconic Irish pub exudes a lively atmosphere, buzzing with karaoke nights, live music, and a wide selection of beers and spirits. It's a great place to mingle with locals and enjoy classic pub fare alongside your drinks.

4. Test Pilot:

Nestled in the heart of the Funk Zone, Test Pilot offers a unique escape. This tropical-themed cocktail lounge transports you to a dreamy setting with its creative and delicious drinks. So, if you're looking for a visually stunning and flavorful experience, Test Pilot is a must-visit.

5. Joe's Café:

A Santa Barbara staple since 1928, Joe's Café seamlessly transforms from a bustling daytime eatery to a lively spot for nighttime revelry. As the sun sets, Joe's transforms, offering an extensive cocktail menu with something to please every palate.

6. EOS Lounge:

For a taste of the Mediterranean, head to EOS Lounge. This vibrant venue features a Mediterranean-inspired atmosphere that transitions from a stylish cocktail bar to a dynamic dance club later in the evening. Immerse yourself in the trendy ambiance and enjoy a night of dancing under the Mediterranean-inspired décor.

7. Shaker Mill:

Shaker Mill offers a unique combination of mid-century tropical vibes and delicious seafood. Enjoy a vibrant cocktail alongside fresh catches from the Broad Street Oyster Co. for a truly memorable evening.

This is just a taste of what Santa Barbara's nightlife has to offer. So, put on your dancing shoes, grab some friends, and explore the diverse options waiting to make your night unforgettable!

Chapter 6: Shopping and Markets

This city beckons with a captivating blend of sunshine, charm, and a vibrant shopping scene. Fashionistas, treasure hunters, and casual browsers alike will find something to tantalize their desires. From iconic brands to hidden boutiques, a diverse selection awaits.

1. State Street Shopping

State Street is the bustling artery of Santa Barbara's shopping scene. Lined with a variety of stores, from high-end retailers to family-owned boutiques, it offers a shopping experience that caters to every taste and budget. Visitors can stroll under the warm California sun as they explore an array of shops offering everything from the latest fashion trends to vintage finds.

2. Boutiques and Unique Shops

Santa Barbara is home to numerous boutiques and unique shops that reflect the city's eclectic and upscale vibe. These shops are often found tucked away in charming side streets and offer exclusive items that can't be found anywhere else. From handcrafted jewelry to bespoke clothing and artisanal home decor, these boutiques are a treasure trove for those looking for something special and one-of-a-kind.

3. Local Markets and Farmers Markets

The local markets and farmer's markets in Santa Barbara are a vibrant showcase of the region's agricultural bounty. These markets are not just a place to buy fresh produce; they're a community gathering spot where locals and visitors alike can enjoy live music, sample gourmet foods, and purchase organic, locally-sourced fruits, vegetables, and other goods. The markets also provide a platform for local farmers and artisans to sell their products directly to consumers.

4. Souvenirs and Local Crafts

For those looking to take a piece of Santa Barbara home with them, the city offers an abundance of souvenirs and local crafts. From hand-painted ceramics to custom surfboards, the range of souvenirs reflects the artistic spirit and coastal lifestyle of Santa Barbara. Local craftspeople take pride in their work, ensuring that each item is not just a souvenir but a work of art that captures the essence of this beautiful city.

Chapter 7: Day Trips and Excursions

Channel Islands National Park

A day trip to Channel Islands National Park offers a unique opportunity to explore one of California's most pristine natural environments. Located just off the coast of Santa Barbara, the park comprises five distinct islands: Anacapa, Santa Cruz, Santa Rosa, San Miguel, and Santa Barbara. Each island boasts its own unique landscapes, wildlife, and recreational opportunities.

Getting There:

To start your adventure, board a ferry from Ventura Harbor, which is the primary gateway to the Channel Islands. The ferry ride itself is a scenic experience, often accompanied by sightings of dolphins, sea lions, and even whales. The ride takes about 1.5 to 2 hours.

Activities:

Upon arrival, a range of activities awaits. Hiking is a popular option, with trails offering stunning coastal views, wildflower meadows, and opportunities to spot native wildlife such as the island fox and numerous bird species. Snorkeling and diving in the clear waters around the islands reveal vibrant underwater ecosystems, including kelp forests and diverse marine life.

Kayaking:

Kayaking is another highlight, particularly around Santa Cruz Island, where you can explore sea caves and coves. Guided kayak tours are available and highly recommended for those unfamiliar with the area.

Wildlife Watching:

Wildlife watching is exceptional, both on land and at sea. The islands are home to several endemic species and are a haven for seabirds. The surrounding waters are rich in marine life, making for excellent opportunities to observe dolphins, seals, and various fish species.

Gearing Up:

Comfortable shoes: Hiking trails are mostly moderate, but sturdy shoes are essential for uneven terrain.

Sunscreen and hat: The California sun can be strong, so pack accordingly.

Water bottle: Stay hydrated! Refillable bottles are best.

Snacks: While some islands offer limited food options, packing snacks ensures you have the energy to explore.

Camera: Capture the stunning scenery and unique wildlife. (Optional: Consider binoculars for birdwatching or spotting marine life)

Plan Ahead:

Be sure to plan your trip in advance, as services on the islands are limited. Bring sufficient water, snacks, and sun protection, and be prepared for rugged terrain. Day trips offer a glimpse into the natural beauty and tranquility of Channel Islands National Park, providing an unforgettable experience for nature lovers and adventure seekers alike.

Santa Ynez Valley and Wine Country

A day trip to the Santa Ynez Valley from Santa Barbara offers a delightful escape into California's celebrated wine country. Just a 45-minute drive from Santa Barbara, this picturesque region is known for its rolling hills, vineyards, and charming small towns.

Getting There:

The scenic drive along Highway 154, also known as the San Marcos Pass, takes you through stunning mountain vistas and oak-studded landscapes, setting the tone for a day of relaxation and exploration.

Wine Tasting:

Santa Ynez Valley is home to over 120 wineries and tasting rooms, each offering a unique experience. Popular stops include the wineries in Los Olivos, a quaint town with numerous tasting rooms within walking distance. For a more immersive experience, head to the vineyards in Ballard Canyon or Foxen Canyon Road, where you can enjoy tours and tastings amid the vines.

Exploring Small Towns:

The valley's charming towns each offer something special. Solvang, known for its Danish-inspired architecture, features bakeries, boutiques, and windmills, making it a fun spot to explore on foot. Los Alamos, with its Old West charm, is another great stop for antique shopping and dining.

Outdoor Activities:

For those who enjoy the outdoors, the valley offers excellent hiking and biking opportunities. The Aliso Canyon and Nojoqui Falls trails provide scenic routes through the countryside. Alternatively, take a leisurely bike ride through the valley's vineyard-lined roads.

Dining:

Enjoy farm-to-table dining at one of the valley's many acclaimed restaurants. Many establishments feature locally sourced ingredients and offer al fresco dining with vineyard views. Picnic areas are also available at several wineries, making it easy to enjoy a relaxing meal amidst the vineyards.

Plan Ahead:

Be sure to plan your winery visits and dining reservations in advance, especially on weekends. Consider joining a guided wine tour for a stress-free experience, allowing you to focus on enjoying the exquisite wines and beautiful scenery without worrying about driving.

A day trip to the Santa Ynez Valley and Wine Country offers a perfect blend of wine tasting, charming towns, and scenic beauty, providing a refreshing and memorable escape from Santa Barbara.

Solvang – The Danish Village

Solvang, affectionately known as the Danish Village, is a charming enclave that offers a taste of Denmark right in California. Just a 45-minute drive from Santa Barbara,

Solvang is a delightful destination for a day trip, where visitors can immerse themselves in Danish culture and architecture.

Exploring the Village: Upon arrival, you can start your exploration at Mission Drive, the main thoroughfare, adorned with Danish windmills and half-timbered houses. Wander through the walkways and shopping nooks, where you'll find a variety of Danish-themed souvenirs, including wooden shoes, cuckoo clocks, and unique clothing.

Danish Culinary Delights: No visit to Solvang is complete without indulging in traditional Danish pastries. Be sure to stop by Paula's Pancake House for their famous Danish pancakes or visit Mortensen's Danish Bakery for a selection of fresh pastries, including the must-try strudel. For chocolate enthusiasts, Rocky Mountain Chocolate Factory offers a wide variety of treats to satisfy your sweet tooth.

Cultural Attractions: Solvang is home to several museums that celebrate its heritage, such as the Elverhøj Museum of History & Art, the Hans Christian Andersen Museum, and the Solvang Vintage Motorcycle Museum. These cultural spots provide insight into the village's history and showcase unique collections.

Festivals and Events: If you're visiting in September, don't miss the Solvang Danish Days, a festival that features a parade, artisan marketplace, Viking-age re-enactments, and an aebleskiver-eating contest. It's a festive time that brings the village's Danish roots to life.

Wine Tasting: Alongside its cultural offerings, Solvang also boasts wine-tasting rooms where visitors can sample local wines, reflecting the region's growing reputation as a wine-producing area.

Theater Under the Stars: End your day with a performance at the Solvang Festival Theater, an outdoor venue that offers live entertainment in a unique setting.

A day trip to Solvang from Santa Barbara promises a blend of cultural immersion, culinary delights, and a touch of whimsy, making it a memorable excursion for you.

Carpinteria

When you're considering a day trip to Carpinteria from Santa Barbara. It's a fantastic little town with a lot to offer, and I'm sure you'll have a great time. Here's what you need to know to make the most of your visit:

Getting There:
- By Car: Carpinteria is just a short 15-minute drive down the iconic Highway 101. The drive itself is part of the experience, with beautiful coastal views along the way.
- By Train: Hop on an Amtrak train for a quick and scenic 15-minute ride. It's an affordable and relaxing way to travel, with tickets costing less than $10 one way.

- By Bus: If you prefer, the city bus is another budget-friendly option, offering a chance to see some of the local sights en route to Carpinteria.

Where to Eat:

- Lucky Llama: Start your day with a coffee or a tasty acai bowl at this local favorite. It's a cozy spot with a lovely outdoor space to relax in.
- Little Dom's Seafood: For lunch or brunch, this place serves up some of the freshest seafood around. They also have a great happy hour and a tempting three-course meal special on Tuesdays.
- The Spot: If you're looking for a quick, delicious, and budget-friendly option, grab a burger here. It's a no-frills joint that's perfect for a casual bite.

What to Do:

- Hit the Beach: Carpinteria City Beach is known as the "World's Safest Beach" and is perfect for a day of sunbathing, swimming, and surfing.

- Nature Trails: There are lovely hiking trails nearby if you want to stretch your legs and enjoy the local flora and fauna.

- Surfboard Rentals: If you're feeling adventurous, rent a surfboard or stand-up paddleboard and hit the waves.

What to See:

- Carpinteria Salt Marsh: Take a walk through this important wetland to spot rare plants and birds.

- Tar Pits State Park: Check out the natural asphalt seeps that have been a part of the landscape for thousands of years.

- Harbor Seal Preserve: Visit the rookery to see the adorable harbor seals lounging along the coastline.

Events:

- California Avocado Festival: If you're in town in October, don't miss this fun-filled festival celebrating all things avocado.

Tips:

- Plan Ahead: Carpinteria is a laid-back town, but it's always good to check the opening hours for any attractions or eateries you want to visit.
- Pack Essentials: Bring sunscreen, a hat, and comfortable walking shoes to fully enjoy your day out.

Carpinteria is a gem of a town with its own unique vibe, and I'm sure you'll find it's the perfect place to unwind and enjoy the California coast.

Chapter 8: Events and Festivals

Annual Events

Santa Barbara's charm goes beyond its stunning beaches. This vibrant coastal city bursts with year-round festivals celebrating everything from culture and heritage to delicious local flavors. It's a rainbow of events for locals and visitors alike!

January

Santa Barbara International Film Festival

Venue: Various locations including Arlington Theatre and Lobero Theatre

The Santa Barbara International Film Festival (SBIFF) is a major event that attracts filmmakers, celebrities, and cinema enthusiasts from around the world. The festival showcases a diverse range of films and includes red carpet events, panels, and workshops.

February

Santa Barbara Restaurant Week

Venue: Various participating restaurants across Santa Barbara

This culinary event celebrates the city's vibrant food scene with special prix-fixe menus offered at local restaurants. It's an excellent opportunity to sample the best of Santa Barbara's cuisine at a variety of price points.

March

Santa Barbara Jewish Film Festival

Venue: The New Vic Theatre

This festival features a selection of Jewish-themed films from around the world, including documentaries, dramas, and comedies. It also includes discussions and Q&A sessions with filmmakers and special guests.

April

Earth Day Festival

Venue: Alameda Park

Santa Barbara's Earth Day Festival is one of the largest and longest-running in the nation. The event includes eco-friendly exhibitors, live music, speakers, and activities focused on sustainability and environmental protection.

Santa Barbara Vintners Spring Weekend

Venue: Various wineries and vineyards in Santa Ynez Valley

This event includes wine tastings, vineyard tours, and special dinners, celebrating the region's winemaking heritage. It's a must-visit for wine enthusiasts looking to experience the best of Santa Barbara's wine country.

May

I Madonnari Italian Street Painting Festival

Venue: Old Mission Santa Barbara

Held over Memorial Day weekend, this festival transforms the plaza in front of the Mission into a vibrant display of chalk art. Artists create intricate and colorful murals on the pavement, while visitors enjoy live music and Italian food.

June

Summer Solstice Parade and Festival

Venue: State Street and Alameda Park

The Summer Solstice Parade is a colorful and whimsical celebration of the longest day of the year. The parade features creative floats, costumes, and performances, followed by a festival in Alameda Park with live music, food, and crafts.

July

California Wine Festival

Venue: Chase Palm Park

This festival showcases California's finest wines alongside gourmet food from local chefs. It includes a beachside tasting event, live music, and an array of culinary delights, making it a favorite summer event for wine lovers.

Old Spanish Days Fiesta

Venue: Various locations including De la Guerra Plaza and Santa Barbara Courthouse

Known simply as "Fiesta," this multi-day event celebrates Santa Barbara's Spanish heritage with parades, traditional music, dance performances, and a variety of cultural activities. Highlights include the El Desfile Histórico parade and the Fiesta Pequeña at the Courthouse.

August

Santa Barbara Greek Festival

Venue: Oak Park

This lively festival celebrates Greek culture with traditional music, dance, and food. Visitors can enjoy authentic Greek cuisine, watch dance performances, and participate in cultural activities.

September

California Lemon Festival

Venue: Girsh Park, Goleta

This family-friendly festival celebrates the region's agricultural history, particularly its lemon orchards. The event includes live entertainment, a classic car show, arts and crafts vendors, and, of course, plenty of lemon-themed treats.

Santa Barbara Harbor & Seafood Festival

Venue: Santa Barbara Harbor

This event showcases the best of Santa Barbara's seafood with fresh catches prepared by local chefs. The festival features cooking demonstrations, live music, and activities for kids, all set against the backdrop of the bustling harbor.

October

Santa Barbara Avocado Festival

Venue: Linden Avenue, Carpinteria

Held in nearby Carpinteria, this festival celebrates all things avocado. It includes avocado-themed foods, live music, and contests, making it a fun and delicious event for all ages.

November

Santa Barbara Veterans Day Parade

Venue: State Street

This parade honors the service and sacrifice of U.S. military veterans. It features marching bands, military vehicles, and veteran groups, culminating in a ceremony at the Veterans Memorial Building.

December

Parade of Lights

Venue: Santa Barbara Harbor

The Parade of Lights is a festive boat parade featuring vessels decorated with holiday lights. The event includes fireworks, a visit from Santa, and activities for families, creating a magical holiday atmosphere along the waterfront.

These annual events reflect Santa Barbara's rich cultural heritage, vibrant community spirit, and stunning natural beauty, offering something for everyone to enjoy throughout the year.

Cultural Festivals

No matter the time of year, Santa Barbara offers a vibrant array of activities for all ages. From wine tasting and film debuts to musical performances, outdoor adventures, food festivals, and art exhibitions, there's an event or festival to suit every taste. Use this helpful guide to plan the perfect getaway to this seaside haven and immerse yourself in the exciting festivals Santa Barbara has to offer!

1. MAY: Taste of Santa Barbara

Indulge in Santa Barbara's renowned culinary scene at the week-long Taste of Santa Barbara. This county-wide extravaganza features insightful discussions, creative pop-ups, film screenings, and farm tours. Foodies will relish tasting events, tributes to culinary icons, and opportunities to connect with local purveyors.

2. MAY: I Madonnari Italian Street Painting Festival

Witness artistic mastery unfold at the I Madonnari Italian Street Painting Festival over Memorial Day weekend. Held at the Old Mission Santa Barbara, the festival transforms the Mission Plaza into a breathtaking open-air gallery. Talented street painters (Madonnari in Italian) create awe-inspiring, large-scale works using colorful pastels. Admission is free, making it a perfect family-friendly outing.

3. JUNE: Santa Barbara Surf Film Festival

Catch the waves (on screen) at the Santa Barbara Surf Film Festival. This two-day event, held at the Lobero Theatre, celebrates the rich history of surfing through captivating films. Explore diverse storytelling styles from filmmakers, artists, board shapers, and legendary surfers. Don't miss the outdoor Surf Film Festival Block Party, featuring local artisans, live music, delicious food, and refreshing craft drinks.

4. JUNE: Juneteenth Santa Barbara Block Party

Commemorate Juneteenth, a national holiday marking the emancipation of enslaved African Americans, at the Santa Barbara Juneteenth Block Party. Held in the Funk Zone, this free event celebrates local Black artists, business owners, performers, and organizations. Enjoy delicious food, vibrant music, and a joyful atmosphere.

5. JUNE: Summer Solstice

Embrace the longest day of the year at the Summer Solstice Parade and Festival. Drawing visitors worldwide, this event is one of the largest art celebrations in Santa Barbara County. Witness vibrant displays of artwork, captivating costumes, and captivating performances. This free festival boasts a special concert event, delectable food options, and local vendors.

6. JUNE: Santa Barbara Greek Festival

Immerse yourself in Greek culture at the highly anticipated Santa Barbara Greek Festival. This year, the festival moves to a new venue – Chase Palm Park –

promising an unforgettable experience. Savor delicious Greek cuisine, including gyros, and sip on chilled Greek beers as you're swept away by the infectious music and lively ambiance.

7. JUNE: Santa Barbara Lavender Festival

Catch the delightful fragrance of lavender at the Santa Barbara Lavender Festival, held at Santa Barbara City College. This free, unique arts and crafts festival celebrates creativity through the lens of lavender. Over 75 local artisans, lavender farms, and small businesses showcase their work, featuring lavender-themed crafts, décor, and products.

8. JULY: California Wine Festival

Wine aficionados rejoice! The California Wine Festival is a two-day extravaganza showcasing the bounty of California's wine regions. Held outdoors, the festival kicks off with an educational seminar and a reserve and rare wine tasting for those seeking a refined experience. On Saturday, the festivities move beachside, featuring over 250 wines from 70 wineries. Local chefs, food purveyors, and artisan vendors complement the offerings. Savor delicious barbecue from Santa Barbara's top restaurants and soak in the cool ocean breeze as you explore the festival's pop-up shops.

9. AUGUST: Old Spanish Days Fiesta

Step back in time and experience Santa Barbara's rich heritage at the Old Spanish Days Fiesta. This granddaddy of city celebrations, dating back to 1925, comes alive during the first week of August. Immerse yourself in the music, dance, and pageantry of this cultural extravaganza. Mark your calendars and plan your ultimate Fiesta experience!

10. AUGUST: Pacific Pride Festival

Celebrate inclusivity and diversity at the Pacific Pride Festival, held at Chase Palm Park towards the end of August, coinciding with Santa Barbara's official Pride Month. This all-day event honors the LGBTQ+ community. Explore booths featuring local food artisans, organizations championing LGBTQ+ rights, and a vibrant selection of arts and crafts.

11. SEPTEMBER: Santa Barbara Studio Artists Open Studios Tour

Labor Day weekend brings the highly anticipated Santa Barbara Studio Artists Open Studios Tour. This renowned event offers a unique opportunity to meet the area's talented artists in their studios and gain a glimpse into their creative process. Don't miss this chance to connect with local artists and discover hidden artistic gems.

12. SEPTEMBER: Santa Barbara Sea Glass & Ocean Arts Festival

Embrace Santa Barbara's connection to the ocean at the Santa Barbara Sea Glass & Ocean Arts Festival. A haven for artisans and crafters, this event celebrates the beauty of ocean-inspired art. Explore gorgeous sea glass jewelry, paintings, sculptures, and other artistic creations crafted from the treasures of the sea. Mark your calendar for this unique showcase of talent.

13. OCTOBER: Santa Barbara Indie Film Fest

Calling all cinema enthusiasts! Head to the historic Alhecama Theatre for the Santa Barbara Indie Film Fest. This two-day celebration showcases a diverse selection of films by independent and youth filmmakers. Network with fellow film lovers and discover the next wave of cinematic brilliance.

14. OCTOBER: Santa Barbara Vintners Festival

Raise a glass to exquisite wines at the Santa Barbara Vintners Festival, held in the picturesque Santa Ynez Valley. This 40-year-old tradition features over 100 wineries alongside culinary delights from Santa Barbara's best chefs. Live music fills the air as you savor exceptional wines and gourmet bites. The festival is complemented by open houses, dinners, and seminars, making it the perfect excuse for a long weekend getaway to wine country.

15. OCTOBER: Santa Barbara Harbor & Seafood Festival

Celebrate the bounty of the sea at the Santa Barbara Harbor & Seafood Festival. Held on the waterfront, this festival is a tribute to hardworking local fisheries. Savor fresh seafood dishes and explore all things marine with boat tours, rides, and dockside demonstrations. Live music and arts and crafts vendors add to the festive atmosphere.

16. OCTOBER: Ride Santa Barbara 100

Calling all cyclists! Gear up for Ride Santa Barbara 100, a premier cycling event offering scenic routes through Santa Barbara County. Choose from various courses catering to all skill levels, from beginner to advanced riders. Challenge yourself and explore the stunning landscapes on two wheels.

17. NOVEMBER: Santa Barbara Jewish Film Festival

Immerse yourself in Jewish culture and identity through film at the Santa Barbara Jewish Film Festival. Held at

The New Vic Theatre, this annual event showcases exceptional films from around the world. Expect documentaries, dramas, comedies, and shorts by American, European, and Israeli filmmakers. The festival dates are typically announced closer to November.

18. NOVEMBER: Santa Barbara Half Marathon

Lace up your running shoes and explore Santa Barbara's scenic coastline at the Santa Barbara Half Marathon. This event welcomes runners and joggers of all ages and abilities, offering a chance to break a sweat and enjoy breathtaking coastal views. It's a perfect way to get some exercise and endorphins before the holiday season arrives.

19. DECEMBER: Parade of Lights

Light up your holidays with the Santa Barbara Parade of Lights. Held on the waterfront, this annual tradition brings festive cheer to the entire family. Witness a dazzling display as more than 30 boats adorned with thousands of twinkling lights and festive decorations illuminate the Santa Barbara Harbor, cruising around Stearns Wharf.

20. FEBRUARY: Santa Barbara International Film Festival

Dress up for a night of glamour at the Santa Barbara International Film Festival (SBIFF). This prestigious event, held every February, is a cinematic smorgasbord. Enjoy a diverse lineup of international films, including new releases, classics, avant-garde pieces, documentaries, and animated and live-action shorts. Panels featuring directors, writers, and producers offer behind-the-scenes insights and industry knowledge. Evening tributes to actors and filmmakers celebrate the stellar work of established and emerging artists – some of whom might even be Oscar-worthy!

21. MARCH: World of Pinot Noir

Calling all wine connoisseurs! The World of Pinot Noir is a delectable celebration dedicated to this exceptional grape varietal. This event brings together pinot noir producers from the most renowned regions worldwide.

Enthusiasts can mingle with these experts and celebrate their passion for pinot noir. The World of Pinot Noir features seminars, lunches, dinners, and the highly sought-after grand tasting event, all hosted at the luxurious Ritz-Carlton Bacara, Santa Barbara.

22. MARCH: Santa Barbara International Orchid Show

Witness a breathtaking display of orchids at the Santa Barbara International Orchid Show. Recognized as one of the country's largest and most prestigious orchid celebrations, this three-day event features over 50 orchid exhibitors and vendors from around the globe. Immerse yourself in a world of vibrant colors, captivating patterns, and unique textures as you explore the vast variety of orchids on display.

23. APRIL: Santa Barbara Bowl

Experience the magic of live music under the stars at the Santa Barbara Bowl. Nestled on a hillside within walking distance of downtown, this historic open-air venue boasts nearly 5,000 seats. A stunning backdrop for musical performances, the Bowl welcomes headliners from every genre, from rock and pop to jazz, mariachi, and classical.

24. APRIL: Earth Day Festival

Celebrate our planet at the Santa Barbara Earth Day Festival. As the birthplace of the very first Earth Day, Santa Barbara takes environmental consciousness seriously. This annual festival is one of the largest on the West Coast, attracting a like-minded community passionate about sustainability. Enjoy live music, indulge in delicious and eco-friendly food and beverage options, and explore informative booths from over 200 exhibitors showcasing sustainable practices.

Music and Arts Festivals

Santa Barbara is a cultural haven, brimming with music and arts festivals that captivate visitors throughout the year. From grand parades to intimate performances, these festivals offer a rich tapestry of artistic expression and celebration.

1. Summer Solstice Parade and Festival (June)

One of the largest art events in Santa Barbara County, the Summer Solstice Parade and Festival draws visitors from around the world. Spectators can expect vibrant displays of artwork, elaborate costumes, dynamic performances, and more. Held on the weekend closest to the summer solstice, this free festival features special concerts, delicious food, and local merchants, creating a lively and colorful celebration of creativity.

2. Santa Barbara Greek Festival (June)

Celebrating its 51st year, the Santa Barbara Greek Festival offers an unforgettable cultural experience. Held at Chase Palm Park, the festival features energetic music from The 4 Greeks, traditional dance performances, and authentic Greek cuisine. Attendees can enjoy chilled Greek beer and delicious gyros while soaking in the festive atmosphere.

3. Santa Barbara International Film Festival (February)

A glittering cinematic event, the Santa Barbara International Film Festival (SBIFF) showcases films from around the globe. Held each February, this festival features a morning-to-night feast of new releases, classics, documentaries, animated films, and avant-garde entries. Panels with directors, writers, and producers offer behind-the-scenes insights, while evening tributes highlight the work of renowned and emerging artists.

4. I Madonnari Italian Street Painting Festival (May)

Held on Memorial Day weekend at Old Mission Santa Barbara, the I Madonnari Italian Street Painting Festival transforms the Mission Plaza into an open-air art gallery. Street painters, known as "Madonnari," create awe-inspiring, large-scale images using pastels, showcasing more than 150 vibrant scenes on the pavement. This free event is open to the public and celebrates the artistry and creativity of the community.

5. Santa Barbara Studio Artists Open Studios Tour (September)

Each Labor Day Weekend, the Santa Barbara Studio Artists' Open Studios Tour provides a unique opportunity to meet the area's talented artists and explore their creative processes. This renowned event allows visitors to tour the studios, engage with the artists, and purchase original works, offering an intimate glimpse into the vibrant local art scene.

6. Parade of Lights (December)

Celebrate the holiday season with Santa Barbara's annual Parade of Lights. Held at the waterfront, this festive event features more than 30 boats adorned with thousands of lights and decorations, creating a magical display as they navigate through the Santa Barbara Harbor and around Stearns Wharf. It's a joyful celebration that brings the entire community together to enjoy the holiday spirit.

These festivals highlight Santa Barbara's rich cultural landscape, offering memorable experiences for all who visit.

Food and Wine Events

Santa Barbara is a haven for food and wine enthusiasts, offering a delightful array of events that celebrate the region's culinary excellence and viticulture.

California Wine Festival: This festival is a love letter to California's winemaking prowess, featuring a collection of fine wines and gourmet foods. It's an outdoor event where you can mingle with winemakers and chefs, all under the sunny Santa Barbara sky.

Santa Barbara Wine & Food Festival: Set along the banks of Mission Creek at the Santa Barbara Museum of Natural History, this festival invites you to enjoy over 100 Central Coast wines. It's a picturesque setting to sip and savor the local flavors, with live entertainment and hors d'oeuvres to enhance the experience.

The Valley Project: Described as a love letter to Santa Barbara's wine country, The Valley Project offers an intimate look at the region's diverse Viticultural Areas.

With soil samples, murals, and wine tastings, it communicates the unique topography, soils, and microclimates of the area.

Djinn: For a more mystical and classy drinking experience, Djinn serves up creative cocktails with a masterful touch. It's a great spot to enjoy the ambiance and the art of mixology.

Chapter 9: Practical Information and Tips

Travel Safety Tips

Santa Barbara is a beautiful and welcoming destination, but like any place, it's important to stay safe while enjoying your visit.

1. Stay Aware of Your Surroundings: Always be mindful of your environment, especially in crowded areas, tourist attractions, and public transportation. Keep an eye on your belongings and avoid distractions that can make you a target for pickpockets.

2. Secure Your Valuables: Use hotel safes to store valuables like passports, extra cash, and electronics. When out and about, carry only what you need for the day and keep important items in a money belt or hidden pouch.

3. Travel in Groups: Whenever possible, explore the city with a companion or in a group, especially at night. There's safety in numbers, and it's often more enjoyable to share experiences with others.

4. Know Emergency Contacts: Familiarize yourself with local emergency numbers. In the United States, the emergency number is 911 for police, fire, and medical assistance.

5. Stay Hydrated and Sun-Safe: Santa Barbara enjoys a sunny climate, so be sure to drink plenty of water, wear sunscreen, and use hats and sunglasses to protect yourself from the sun's rays.

6. Be Cautious with Strangers: While Santa Barbara is generally safe, it's wise to be cautious when interacting with strangers. Avoid sharing too much personal information and be wary of offers that seem too good to be true.

7. Use Reliable Transportation: Opt for reputable transportation services such as licensed taxis, rideshare apps, or public transit. If you're renting a car, ensure it's from a well-known rental company and familiarize yourself with the local driving laws.

8. Keep Digital Copies of Important Documents: Make digital copies of your passport, ID, travel insurance, and itinerary. Store these copies securely online so you can access them if the originals are lost or stolen.

9. Stay Informed About Local Conditions: Check local news and weather reports for any updates that might affect your travel plans. Pay attention to advisories regarding natural events like wildfires, which can occur in California.

10. Follow Health Guidelines: Stay informed about current health guidelines, especially in light of recent global health concerns. Carry a mask and hand sanitizer, and practice good hygiene.

11. Respect Local Laws and Customs: Familiarize yourself with local laws and cultural norms to ensure a respectful and lawful visit. This includes understanding traffic laws, smoking regulations, and rules at natural sites.

12. Stay in Well-Lit and Populated Areas: Stick to well-lit, populated areas, especially at night. Avoid walking alone in unfamiliar or poorly lit places.

By following these safety tips, you can enjoy a worry-free visit to Santa Barbara and make the most of your time in this picturesque seaside city.

Useful Contacts and Emergency Information

Some useful contacts and emergency information for anyone visiting Santa Barbara:

Emergency Services

- Emergency Number (Police, Fire, Medical): 911
- Non-Emergency Police: (805) 882-8900
- Santa Barbara County Fire Department: (805) 681-5500

Medical Services

- Santa Barbara Cottage Hospital:
  - Address: 400 W Pueblo St, Santa Barbara, CA 93105
  - Phone: (805) 682-7111
- Sansum Clinic Urgent Care:
  - Address: 215 Pesetas Ln, Santa Barbara, CA 93110
  - Phone: (805) 563-6110
- Marian Regional Medical Center:
  - Address: 1400 E Church St, Santa Maria, CA 93454
  - Phone: (805) 739-3000

Visitor Information

- Visit Santa Barbara:

  - Address: 500 E Montecito St, Santa Barbara, CA 93103

  - Phone: (805) 966-9222

  - Website: (santabarbaraca)

- Santa Barbara Visitor Center:

  - Address: 1 Garden St, Santa Barbara, CA 93101

  - Phone: (805) 965-3021

Transportation

- Santa Barbara Airport:

  - Address: 500 James Fowler Rd, Santa Barbara, CA 93117

  - Phone: (805) 683-4011

- Amtrak Santa Barbara Station:

  - Address: 209 State St, Santa Barbara, CA 93101

  - Phone: (800) 872-7245

- Santa Barbara MTD (Public Transit):

  - Customer Service: (805) 963-3366

  - Website: (sbmtd.gov)

Consular Services

- Consulate General of Mexico in Oxnard:
  - Address: 3151 W 5th St, Oxnard, CA 93030
  - Phone: (805) 984-8738
- British Consulate General Los Angeles:
  - Address: 2029 Century Park E #1350, Los Angeles, CA 90067
  - Phone: (310) 789-0031

Lost & Found

- Santa Barbara Airport Lost & Found:
  - Phone: (805) 681-4312
- Santa Barbara MTD Lost & Found:
  - Phone: (805) 963-3366
- Amtrak Lost & Found:
  - Phone: (800) 872-7245

Utilities and Services

- Southern California Edison (Electricity):
  - Customer Service: (800) 655-4555
- Southern California Gas Company:
  - Customer Service: (800) 427-2200

- City of Santa Barbara Water Services:
  - Customer Service: (805) 564-5343

Local Weather and Road Conditions

- National Weather Service Santa Barbara:
  - Website: (weather.gov)
- California Highway Patrol (CHP) Road Conditions:
  - Phone: (800) 427-7623
  - Website: (dot.ca.gov)

Having these contacts and information at hand will help ensure a safe and enjoyable visit to Santa Barbara.

Maps for Navigation

Scan the above QR code for Santa Barbara map

Conclusion

Santa Barbara truly offers something for everyone, with its rich blend of cultural events, breathtaking natural beauty, and a welcoming community spirit. Whether you're savoring local wines, exploring vibrant festivals, indulging in world-class cuisine, or simply soaking up the sun on pristine beaches, this seaside haven promises an unforgettable experience. Use this guide to navigate the myriad of activities and attractions, ensuring your visit is as seamless and enjoyable as possible. From the scenic landscapes to the bustling arts scene, Santa Barbara awaits with endless adventures and cherished memories just waiting to be made. Safe travels and enjoy your stay!

Made in the USA
Columbia, SC
16 April 2025

56698766R00080